T0193935

THE PSYCHOLOGY OF ARTIFICIAL INTELLIGENCE

What is Artificial Intelligence? How will AI impact society? Is AI more powerful than human intelligence?

The Psychology of AI explores all aspects of the psychology-AI relationship, asking how closely AI can resemble humans and whether this means they could have some form of self-awareness. It considers how AI systems have been modelled on human intelligence and the similarities between brains and computers, along with the current limitations of AI and how these could be overcome in the future. It also looks at how people interact with AI in their everyday lives, exploring some of the ethical and societal risks, such as bias in AI algorithms and the consequences for our long-term future if AIs surpass humans in important ways.

As AI continues to break new milestones, The Psychology of AI answers key questions about what it really means to be human and how AI will impact our lives in every way, now and into the future.

Tony Prescott is Professor of Cognitive Robotics at the University of Sheffield, UK. He holds a PhD in Machine Learning and is a Fellow of the British Psychological Society. He is the lead editor of Living Machines: A Handbook of Research in Biomimetics and Biohybrid Systems (OUP, 2018) and Scholarpedia of Touch (Springer, 2017). He has authored over two hundred and fifty articles and conference papers in the areas of psychology, computational neuroscience, robotics, and machine learning.

THE PSYCHOLOGY OF EVERYTHING

People are fascinated by psychology, and what makes humans tick. Why do we think and behave the way we do? We've all met armchair psychologists claiming to have the answers, and people that ask if psychologists can tell what they're thinking. The Psychology of Everything is a series of books which debunk the popular myths and pseudo-science surrounding some of life's biggest questions.

The series explores the hidden psychological factors that drive us, from our subconscious desires and aversions, to our natural social instincts. Absorbing, informative, and always intriguing, each book is written by an expert in the field, examining how research-based knowledge compares with popular wisdom, and showing how psychology can truly enrich our understanding of modern life.

Applying a psychological lens to an array of topics and contemporary concerns—from sex, to fashion, to conspiracy theories—The Psychology of Everything will make you look at everything in a new way.

Titles in the series:

For more information about this series, please visit: www.routledge textbooks.com/textbooks/thepsychologyofeverything/

THE PSYCHOLOGY OF ARTIFICIAL INTELLIGENCE

TONY PRESCOTT

Routledge
Taylor & Francis Group

LONDON AND NEW YORK

Designed cover image: ©Getty Images

First published 2025
by Routledge
4 Park Square, Milton Park, Abingdon, Oxon OX14 4RN

and by Routledge
605 Third Avenue, New York, NY 10158

Routledge is an imprint of the Taylor & Francis Group, an informa business

British Library Cataloguing-in-Publication Data
A catalogue record for this book is available from the British Library

Library of Congress Cataloging-in-Publication Data
Names: Prescott, Tony J., author.
Title: The psychology of artificial intelligence / Tony J. Prescott.
Description: Abingdon, Oxon ; New York, NY : Routledge, 2024. |
    Series: The psychology of everything | Includes bibliographical
    references.
Identifiers: LCCN 2024001236 (print) | LCCN 2024001237
    (ebook) | ISBN 9780367543105 (hardback) | ISBN
    9780367543112 (paperback) | ISBN 9781003088660 (ebook)
Subjects: LCSH: Artificial intelligence—Psychological aspects. |
    Artificial intelligence—Social aspects. | Artificial intelligence—
    Moral and ethical aspects.
Classification: LCC Q334.7 .P74 2024 (print) | LCC Q334.7
    (ebook) | DDC 006.301—dc23/eng/20240123
LC record available at https://lccn.loc.gov/2024001236
LC ebook record available at https://lccn.loc.gov/2024001237

ISBN: 978-0-367-54310-5 (hbk)
ISBN: 978-0-367-54311-2 (pbk)
ISBN: 978-1-003-08866-0 (ebk)

DOI: 10.4324/9781003088660

Typeset in Joanna
by Apex CoVantage, LLC

For my parents, John and Diana

CONTENTS

1

INTRODUCTION

Artificial Intelligence, or AI for short, is "the science and engineering of making intelligent machines, especially intelligent computer programs".[1] This is according to John McCarthy, one of the founders of the field, who adds that AI is "related to the similar task of using computers to understand human intelligence, but AI does not have to confine itself to methods that are biologically observable".[2]

This book is about artificial intelligence and its relationship to the science of understanding human intelligence—*psychology*. This is a complex, multiway relationship. First, as McCarthy suggests, because psychology and AI have similar subject matters, both are concerned with intelligence. Psychology studies intelligence in its natural form, as seen in humans and animals. AI is concerned with the possibility of creating synthetic (human-made) intelligence in artefacts, particularly computers, but also artefacts that might more closely resemble animals, such as robots.

As we will explore, some psychologists, also known as cognitive scientists, use AI methods to create and test theories of human intelligence. Researchers in AI also look to borrow ideas from psychology and neuroscience—the scientific understanding of brains and nervous systems—to create new forms of AI. Although AI is not limited to copying natural intelligence, when it follows a different path, we sometimes call that *alien AI*. Due to this two-way sharing of ideas and

DOI: 10.4324/9781003088660-1

insights, AI and psychology have been intertwined since the earliest days of computers. Indeed, the idea of thinking machines is almost as old as Psychology itself, beginning with the early Greek thinkers.

There are further ways in which psychology is relevant to AI. One is that, as AIs come into the world, people will interact with them, and they will change society and how we live. Understanding how AI will impact humans and how people will relate to AIs, including physical ones such as robots, has led to new fields of research known as *human-machine interaction* and *user experience*.

Psychological methods are also being used to understand how people see AI, for example, our attitudes towards AI and our thoughts and fears about how AI might impact us in the future. Of course, AI is already here, so some of these impacts are already happening, but people are also thinking and are concerned about the longer term. For example, could AI become *superintelligent*, and if so, what would happen next? This idea, sometimes called the *AI singularity*, is hotly debated, both as to whether it might happen and whether the outcome (for humanity) would be good or bad, or even very, very bad, to the point where humans are replaced by AIs as imagined in some science fiction movies.

All of these aspects of the psychology–AI relationship will be explored in this short book.

Chapter 2 will look at the nature of intelligence so that we have a clear idea of what it could mean to create intelligent artefacts. We will look at different aspects of intelligence in people and consider whether intelligence is one thing or many.

Chapter 3 will look at the similarities and differences between brains and computers. After all, AI is predicated on the idea that computers are like brains in important ways, allowing both to be intelligent. We will explore the extent to which this is the case.

Chapter 4 will look at some of the building blocks of intelligent systems, both natural and artificial, from different kinds of reasoning and control, through processes such as search and optimisation. We will ask whether humans think differently from machines and explore unsolved challenges, including the role of emotions in decision-making.

Chapter 5 investigates brain-inspired AIs called *neural networks* that are designed to be especially good at learning. We will explore how the latest *deep neural networks* are being developed to address some of the most challenging problems in AI, including the especially human capacity of language.

Chapter 6 considers *artificial general intelligence* (AGI), a form of AI that is as flexible and general-purpose as human intelligence. We will look at the current limitations of AI, compared to human intelligence, and whether AIs could better understand the world if provided with robotic bodies. We will also discuss how the development of the current class of predictive AIs is leading to new theories of human intelligence.

Finally, in Chapter 7, we will look at how people can live alongside AI, including our attitudes towards AI and our possible relationships with it. This chapter will also consider some of the ethical and societal risks, such as bias and error in AI algorithms, and the consequences for our long-term future as AIs surpass human intelligence in important ways.

A consideration throughout will be the question of how closely AIs can resemble humans. If they can think like we do, does this mean they could have some form of self-awareness? If so, where does that leave us? Are we the biological equivalent of very complex robots? We will pose these questions rather than provide a full answer here. However, this does illustrate that the relationship between psychology and AI gets close to the heart of what we are as thinking beings and points to the possibility of a deeper understanding of what it means to be human.

NOTES

1 Quote retrieved from http://jmc.stanford.edu/artificial-intelligence/what-is-ai/index.html.
2 Ibid.

2

WHAT IS INTELLIGENCE?

When you think about it, artificial intelligence might easily have been called something else. For instance, it could be characterised as the quest to create "artificial psychology"[1] or to build "synthetic minds".[2] Minds are more obviously multifaceted things, whereas there is an idea that intelligence might just be one key thing and that when we figure that out, the challenge of AI will be solved. Here, we will look at the origins of research in AI and how we came to think of building AI. We will also look at the emergence of the idea of intelligence in psychology and whether intelligence is one thing or many.

THE ORIGINS OF AI

Intelligent machines have been imagined for more than a thousand years. Machines that could surprise people with their seemingly intelligent behaviour began appearing in the 17th century in the form of clockwork automata. These included a duck made of copper that appeared to eat and digest and a mechanical flute player made from wood.[3] Charles Babbage brought AI a step closer to reality in the 19th century with his idea for the first programmable digital computer, provoking his friend Ada Lovelace to argue against the possibility of machine creativity. "The Analytical Engine [Babbage's computer]", Lovelace wrote, "has no pretensions whatever to originate anything. It can do whatever we know how to order it to perform".[4]

DOI: 10.4324/9781003088660-2

In the first half of the 20th century, beginning with thinkers such as the mathematician Norbert Wiener[5] and the psychiatrist Ross Ashby,[6] much of the research that we might now call AI went by the name *cybernetics*. This term comes from the Greek word *kubernētēs*, meaning to act as a pilot or helmsman. The ideas of the cyberneticians placed emphasis on the role of a *controller*, that is, a decision-making mechanism embedded in a feedback loop (see Figure 2.1) within which it senses the world and generates appropriate actions.

In the 1940s, Ashby designed and demonstrated a physical device called the *Homeostat* that incorporated many cybernetic principles, including Ashby's law of "requisite variety"—that a machine must be at least as complex as the system it controls if it is to be stable in the face of change. Cybernetics reminds us that intelligence does not happen in isolation. We are intelligent to the extent that we act appropriately in the environment that we live in, maintain ourselves, and (hopefully) achieve our personal goals. The idea of intelligence as control has not gone away, and we will explore it later in this book.

The term "artificial intelligence" only really took off after a now-famous research meeting in the mid-1950s. A young researcher, John McCarthy, who had just been appointed to his first academic post, organised an eight-week retreat, to which McCarthy, with the help of some leading visionaries, managed to recruit some of the most active and well-known researchers with interests in building smart

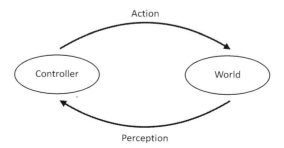

Figure 2.1 The cybernetic idea of an intelligent controller that is in a closed loop with the world.

machines. In proposing the workshop for funding, the term *artificial intelligence* was chosen, perhaps partly to promote the novelty of this enterprise relative to the existing field of cybernetics:

> We propose that a 2-month, 10-man study of artificial intelligence be carried out during the summer of 1956 at Dartmouth College in Hanover, New Hampshire. The study is to proceed on the basis of the conjecture that every aspect of learning or any other feature of intelligence can in principle be so precisely described that a machine can be made to simulate it.[7]

In the end, more than twenty people, and perhaps as many as forty, attended the workshop, though some for just a few days. On most days, this mix of engineers, mathematicians, cyberneticians, and psychologists met on the top floor of the Dartmouth mathematics building and held lively discussions on different topics. The themes considered included the theory of computing, natural language, neural networks, creativity, and abstraction, all of which are still core research topics for AI today, and some will be featured later in this book.

After the participants dispersed, many went on to get substantial research funding to advance the new field of AI. Some believed that the development of machines that could match human intelligence would be possible in their own lifetimes. For instance, in 1960, Herb Simon, a key participant at Dartmouth, a leading AI theorist, and already a Nobel prize winner in economics, wrote that "machines will be capable, within twenty years, of doing any work that a man can do".[8] Interviewed in *Life* magazine in 1970, Marvin Minsky, one of the co-organisers of the retreat, suggested that "in from three to eight years we will have a machine with the general intelligence of an average human being . . . at that point it will be able to educate itself at fantastic speed",[9] and, more ominously, that "if we're lucky, they [the AIs] might decide to keep us as pets".[10] As we will see, these predictions did not quite play out, though in the 2020s, the term artificial intelligence is more popular than ever, and there is (again) no shortage of notable researchers predicting that AIs will soon surpass humans in all respects.

So, we are stuck, for better or worse, with AI as the label for efforts to make machines that think. As we can see from McCarthy's definition at the beginning of Chapter 1, AI is the science and engineering of building intelligent machines. However, this rather begs the question, what do we mean by intelligence? Partly to side-step this challenge, AI is often defined in relation to intelligence of the human variety; that is, whatever it is that we humans do that is seen as requiring intelligence. Of course, this does not explain intelligence either; rather, it passes the buck to the science of human behaviour—psychology.

COMPARING HUMANS WITH AIs

This comparison with humans suggests that whatever intelligence is, we know it when we see it. Humans are *Homo sapiens*—the wise hominid—distinctive for our large brains, capacity for tool use and language, and our invention of a technological culture. Though other animals are intelligent, sometimes in different ways, human intelligence has always been seen as the key benchmark for AI.

This idea led Alan Turing, one of the founders of computer science, to propose a test of whether machines can think, originally named the "imitation game"[11] but now universally known as the *Turing test*. Specifically, Turing proposed that we can judge whether a machine is truly intelligent by setting it against a person in a question-answer session. In his game, any question on any topic is put, in written form only, to both the AI (usually a chatbot) and the human. A second person, typically someone with relevant expertise and experience, is asked to assess which answer came from the human and which from the artefact. If the success of the judge is no better than guesswork (50% correct), then, according to Turing, we should agree that the machine is intelligent or "can think" to use Turing's precise phrase.

Turing proposed his test in 1950. Since then, it has been the subject of many articles, and multiple competitions have been organised to measure AI's success in this game. One such competition, the

Loebner Prize, ran from 1990 through to 2019 but never awarded its ultimate prize of £100,000. This prize could only be won by an AI deemed to have "passed" the test as assessed by a panel of distinguished judges.

The philosopher John Searle, in a famous series of papers describing a "Chinese Room" thought experiment,[12] argued that even if an AI were to pass the Turing test, this would still not be proof of machine intelligence since a machine might pass the test without having any real understanding. Searle's argument has been hugely influential, so it is important to recount it here.

Searle, as a non-Chinese speaker, imagines himself inside a special room whose purpose is to answer questions in Chinese. Chinese speakers outside the room ask questions by writing them on postcards and posting them under the door. To answer them, Searle uses a book of rules written in English but designed specifically for answering questions in Chinese. By carefully following these rules, Searle is able to translate questions composed of Chinese characters—to him, sequences of meaningless "squiggles"—into answers that are also in Chinese. He provides his answers by posting them back under the door.

Searle imagines that the rules he is following are sufficiently comprehensive that, to the outside observers, his answers can be taken for those of a native Chinese speaker. In other words, the Chinese Room can pass this variant of Turing's famous test. However, Searle maintains that he (Searle in the room) understands nothing about Chinese; he is just mechanically following rules. Similarly, an AI, by following a sufficiently sophisticated program, might pass an actual Turing test but understand nothing about the meaning of the answers it was generating. For Searle, this simple thought experiment was proof that the Turing test was not an adequate test of human-level intelligence and that "programs are neither constitutive of, nor sufficient for, minds".[13]

The Chinese Room critique is highly pertinent today when modern chatbots such as OpenAI's *ChatGPT* surprise us with their ability to write and converse in a very human-like way. A dispute is raging as to whether this is a form of "true" intelligence or whether ChatGPT and other recent AIs are, like Searle in the Chinese Room, giving an appearance of intelligence while lacking any genuine understanding. We will explore this question further in Chapter 6.

To the vexation of some AI researchers, behavioural yardsticks for intelligence, of which the conversational capacity required to pass the Turing test is an example, also seem to change over time. For instance, skill at chess playing was once seen as a key benchmark for human-level smarts. However, computers have been beating human grandmasters in chess since 1996 when the IBM chess computer, *Deep Blue*, defeated the then chess world champion Garry Kasparov in a six-match series. A series of computer programs developed by *Google DeepMind*, have, in more recent years, triumphed over human champions in the even more intractable game of Go. However, success in game-playing is now seen as a less important indicator than it used to be. These days, critics of AI are more likely to point to emotional intelligence and to highlight capacities such as creativity rather than expertise in game-playing, deductive thinking, theorem proving, and so on, where AI has had significant success. This could be seen as either "moving the goalposts" or as finding out what the challenging aspects of human intelligence really are.

So just imitating aspects of human intelligence may not be enough to satisfy some of those who are sceptical about thinking machines. Should we perhaps try, instead, to remove some of the gaps in our definitions and to be more specific about what being intelligent entails?

John McCarthy proposed that intelligence is "the computational part of the ability to achieve goals in the world". This may help a little, reminding us, as emphasised by cyberneticians, that intelligence does not exist in a vacuum but is part of a loop that allows us to take action in the world. However, the keyword *computation* is doing a lot of heavy lifting here. What exactly does that mean? We will come back to this question and to what, if anything, brains "compute" in Chapter 3. First, though, let us look a bit more closely at human intelligence to see if that can provide a better description of what we should be looking for.

THE ORIGINS OF THE IDEA OF INTELLIGENCE

Our modern English word "intelligence" comes from the Latin *intelligentia*, which, in turn, has two roots, *inter* meaning *between*, and *legere*—to pick out or read. In other words, it means something like "to choose between", reminding us of the role of intelligence in determining effective action.

The philosopher Aristotle, who lived in the 4th century BCE, is often regarded as the father of psychology and the person to whom we owe the distinction between perception and intelligence. For Aristotle, *aesthesis* or perception—seeing, hearing, touching, tasting, and so on—was the capacity that distinguished animals from plants, all animals having at least a sense of touch. In contrast, only humans had *nuos*—which is usually translated as intelligence, intellect, or mind.[14]

Aristotle's distinction was reinforced during the 17th century by the philosopher René Descartes, famous for his dualist view of mind and body. For a dualist (note, not someone who fights duels!) mind and body are fundamentally different kinds of things, with the mind existing outside the physical realm to which the body belongs. For Descartes, the mind was unique to humans and was the seat of reason, while the body was the realm of the senses. Whilst the mind could be trusted ("cogito ergo sum"—I think; therefore, I exist), the body was a potential source of deception. Indeed, in one of his writings, Descartes imagined an evil demon that manipulated the senses to provide false impressions of the external world.[15]

Modern psychology raises questions about the intelligence–perception distinction. Of course, it is evident now that most animals do more than just perceive and that there is much more continuity between human and animal intelligence than Aristotle or Descartes may have realised. However, more problematically, if we look at how nervous systems work, the distinction between perception and intellect is also fuzzy. As we will see in Chapter 3, nervous systems are built from specialist cells called *neurons*. There are *sensory* neurons that directly encode stimuli from the world, such as the light-sensitive neurons that line the interior of the eyeball, and there are *motor* neurons that directly stimulate muscles to create movement. Between the sensory and motor cells, all other neurons in the nervous system, the vast majority, are *interneurons* and are doing something a bit different. Even the simplest animals with nervous systems, such as *Hydra*—a small freshwater organism with a tubular body and tentacles but no brain—have nerve nets that include neurons that are neither sensory nor motor but connect the two in some complex mesh.

When we look at mammalian and human brains, it is possible to label areas as primarily sensory or perceptual and others as primarily motor. But this is a broad brush. Sensory areas can be seen to be involved in choosing actions, for example, and motor areas can receive and process sensory signals. For areas of the brain that seem to be neither, the terminology can be quite loose. For example, most of the *cerebral cortex* of the human brain, which is made up of left and right cerebral *cortices*, is labelled as "associative" (see Figure 2.2, left). This is another term we owe to Aristotle, who proposed that learning involved the *association*, or linking, of mental concepts.

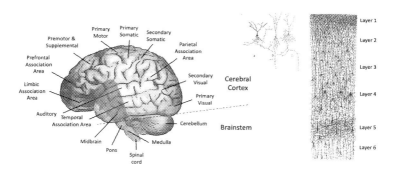

Figure 2.2 *Left.* A side-on view of the human brain (the front is towards the left) showing some widely used labels and the division into the cerebral cortex and the brainstem. Note that the brainstem (shown by the darker, shaded region) extends inside the cortical mantle. *Centre and right.* Three example cortical neurons and the six-layer neural network found in a typical cortical column as drawn by the neuroscientist Santiago Ramón y Cajal, who pioneered the microscopic study of the brain.

When we look closely at these associative areas, we find a very wide variety of mental processes for which psychology has developed additional labels. For instance, there are areas thought to be involved in motivation, emotion, language, reasoning, planning, navigation, decision-making, and so on. However, this labelling is not clearly settled, and many areas seem to contribute to different aspects of function, just as different functions seem to be spread across many areas of the brain. The brain, it seems, has not evolved in a way that is easy for scientists to interpret!

Even if we could agree that parts of the brain can be distinguished as being principally perceptual/motor or other (intellect), when we look at these different brain areas in more detail, they are all made of similar stuff. For example, all of human cortex, be it sensory, motor, or associative, is made up of six-layered neural networks laid out in local patches called columns (see Figure 2.2, right, and next chapter). Neuroscientists agree that these columns have a similar network architecture—the way the neurons are wired to each other—regardless of where they are found. Although there are local differences, and critically, the detailed wiring is subject to adjustment and learning during development, what seems to matter most is how these patches connect to each other and, ultimately, to sensory inputs and motor outputs. This commonality of mechanism suggests that the problems of perception and intellect may not be as different as originally thought.

Despite these issues, Aristotle's distinction between perception and intellect continues to shape how people commonly think about minds and brains. For example, we are more likely to conceive of people as varying in their intellectual capacity, even though there is plentiful evidence of individuals with exceptional sensory capacities, such as so-called "super tasters" who can discriminate many more flavours than the rest of us. Likewise, we recognise that some people can have exceptional sensory and motor capacities, such as the ability to strike a football particularly well. Nevertheless, we are less likely, culturally, to consider this to be a sign of exceptional intellect, even though such skills undoubtedly involve much more of the brain than just those parts that process signals from the eye or drive movement of the legs and feet.[16]

INTELLIGENCE AND IQ TESTING

A key idea that comes from psychology and often leads us to think of intelligence as "one thing" is IQ or the *intelligence quotient*. The capacity to measure IQ, and thus, potentially, to quantify human intelligence, is one of the best-known achievements of a research area in psychology known as *individual differences* or *differential psychology*. If we have a measure of intelligence, does that not imply that we know what it is? Well, not really.

We owe the IQ test to an ingenious psychologist, Alfred Binet,[17] working at the start of the 20th century. At the behest of the French Ministry for Education, Binet wanted to identify children who were performing poorly in class, particularly those who might benefit from special schooling. Binet's idea was to bring together many short tasks or puzzles drawn from everyday life that, besides requiring the ability to read, would not rely on any formal education. For example, a task might ask you to identify the missing portion of a symmetric pattern, find a missing number in a sequence, or solve arithmetic riddles such as: "Peter, who is twelve, is three times his brother's age. How old will Peter be when he is twice the age of his brother?" (You can find the answer at the end of this chapter in case you are wondering).

Whereas earlier approaches to measuring intellect had focused on specific abilities, Binet's intention was to measure many different aspects of thinking and reasoning in the hope that a summary score would reflect the student's overall capability. Binet also arranged his tasks in order of increasing difficulty, rating each one according to the chronological age at which a typical child should be able to perform it. By asking a child to work through the sequence until they could no longer perform a task successfully, Binet was able to estimate what he called the child's mental age. Subtracting mental age from chronological age gave a measure of how a child was performing relative to his peer group.

It is notable that Binet did not start with a definition of intelligence; indeed, quite the opposite, he opted for a large number and wide range of tasks, suggesting "it matters very little what the tests are as long as they are numerous".[18] This approach avoided the problem of saying exactly what it was he was trying to measure. Binet created three versions of his test during his lifetime. In 1912, shortly after Binet's death, William Stern suggested dividing mental age by chronological age (rather than subtracting), leading to the measure we now call the *intelligence quotient*. The notion of IQ and the IQ test was born.

IQ testing has been, and still is, very widely applied. However, it has also had a chequered history. Arguably, the misapplication of IQ testing has led to reduced life chances for many rather than the improvement in education practices that Binet had hoped for. For example, the culture of IQ testing has led, in some parts of the world, to the exclusion of many children from access to education and to the invention of unfortunate labels, such as "moron", for people with low IQ scores.

Although Binet considered that he was measuring a wide range of intellectual abilities and that children with lower scores could improve on his tests by extra schooling, a profoundly different view took hold in psychological circles in the first half of the 20th century. Based on limited and controversial evidence, this view determined that the capacity to perform well on IQ tests was decided through heredity rather than experience. That is, IQ was thought to measure your intellectual endowment that education could do little to change.

Still more controversially, some researchers asserted that differences in IQ could explain differences in social status—for instance, that the poor and underprivileged are so because of lower intelligence. Finally, some large-scale studies of IQ appeared to show differences in average IQ between ethnic groups. Such findings were seized upon by political factions to justify economic inequality or the supposed superiority of one race to others. Many of these studies can be criticised for the failure to control for differences in diet, education, and life chances of the different groups studied. Cultural factors in some of the tasks included in IQ tests also made those tasks easier for some people than others. The many flaws in theories of intelligence based on IQ testing are explored in the book *The Mismeasure of Man* by Stephen J. Gould.[19]

Alongside these socially divisive effects of some IQ studies, attempts to measure intelligence via IQ testing have cemented, in Western culture, the idea that IQ tests measure the strength of a general intellectual faculty akin to Aristotle's *nuos*. When, in 1994, Richard Hernstein and Charles Murray published their book "The Bell Curve",[20] they summarised one popular assessment of almost one hundred years of research on intelligence assessment: that intelligence is a single monolithic capacity that you are largely born with, and that varies across the population with most people near to the average and a smaller number towards each of the extremes (the "bell curve" of the title).

MULTIPLE INTELLIGENCES

This view of intelligence as a single faculty remains popular in academic psychology, as it is in wider society, but there are alternative schools of thought.

In the field of IQ testing, researchers quickly developed sub-scales for different aspects of intelligence. Today if you perform an IQ test, such as the *Weschler Adult Intelligence Scale* (WAIS), you can be given separate scores for verbal comprehension, working memory, perceptual organisation, and processing speed, alongside your overall IQ. Whereas testing of this kind can yield differences for individuals on different sub-scales, it is always possible to take an average—your IQ. It is also the case that scores on sub-scales correlate highly with each other and with the overall measure; that is, people with high scores on one sub-scale tend, on average, to have high scores on others. This, by itself, does not show that there is one thing we should call intelligence, as we will explore shortly. David Weschler, writing about the WAIS test, which he developed, described intelligence as an "aggregate or global capacity of the individual to act purposefully, to think rationally, and to deal effectively with his environment".[21] This definition leaves open the idea that intelligence is more than one thing (an "aggregate").

In the 20th century, several notable psychologists explored what might be called a multiple intelligences view. For instance, Robert Sternberg[22] proposed a *triarchic* theory of intelligence. One kind, *analytical* intelligence, corresponds to the kind of problem-solving measured in traditional IQ tests. But Sternberg also argued for a capacity for *creative* intelligence, the ability to deal with new situations in a successful and appropriate way, and for *practical* intelligence, the capacity to cope with concrete, real-life challenges.

The cognitive scientist Howard Gardner[23] has also proposed a multiple intelligences view, noting that people have different talents and that being good at one thing does not guarantee being good at another. Gardner's list of intelligences includes *linguistic*, *logico-mathematical*, and *spatial* intelligences—again, abilities similar to those measured by traditional intelligence tests. To these, Gardner added intelligences more associated with the creative arts; these included *musical* and *bodily-kinaesthetic* (as might be used in sport, dancing, or acting) intelligences. Finally, at least in Gardner's original list, he included *intrapersonal* intelligence, the capacity to understand and plan effectively for oneself, and *interpersonal* intelligence, the ability to understand others, including reasoning about their feelings, goals, and intentions.

The idea of a distinct faculty for interpersonal or *social* intelligence has a long pedigree. For instance, writing in 1920, Edward Thorndike, a psychologist best known for his contributions to understanding learning, proposed that intelligence had distinct mechanical, abstract, and social components.[24]

Another form of intelligence overlooked by traditional intelligence measures is *emotional* intelligence. As highlighted in an influential 1990 article by Peter Salovey and John Mayer,[25] this relates to our capacity to monitor our own feelings and to use this in a discriminative way to guide decision-making. The importance of attending to our feelings in making wise decisions has also been explored by the neuropsychologist Antonio Damasio,[26] who looked at the poor life decisions sometimes made by people with damage to the emotional parts of the brain. The science journalist Daniel Goleman further popularised this idea in a best-selling book,[27] arguing that emotional intelligence, including capacities such as self-regulation and empathy, is critical to success in life. A related contrast, proposed by the psychologist Daniel Kahneman,[28] known for his work on economic decision-making, is between two systems underlying "fast" and "slow" thinking. The fast system is automatic, emotional, and often instinctive and unconscious. The slow system is deliberate, conscious, effortful, and requires logic and reasoning.

What are we to make of all these different kinds of intelligence? There are several possibilities. One is that there is a single underlying *general* ability alongside several *specific* abilities related to these different aspects of intelligence. Following Charles Spearman[29]—one of the first people to investigate these relationships statistically—psychologists often call these g and s. According to this theory, each specific ability, s, is partly due to general intelligence, g, and partly due to processes unique to that intelligence. This proposal is illustrated by the left-hand Venn diagram in Figure 2.3.

Psychologists, such as Spearman, inferred that the similarity in scores for different IQ sub-tests is caused by the presence of a hidden causal process, g, or general intelligence. This is one result that is consistent with a powerful statistical method, also invented by Spearman, called *factor analysis*, that has been used ever since to look for patterns in intelligence-testing data. However, the right-hand Venn diagram in Figure 2.3 could also be consistent with scores on the different

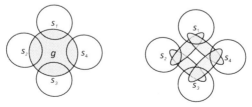

Figure 2.3 Two alternative models of how general intelligence could influence specific intelligences. *Left*. A single general ability (g, darker circle) is inferred to be involved in all specific intelligences. *Right*. This model suggests the presence of multiple underlying processes (grey ovals) with no two specific intelligences involving the same set of hidden processes.

sub-tests being similar. Here, I have illustrated the idea that there might not be just one underlying hidden process but several. Each specific intelligence is influenced by two of these processes in this example, but no one underlying process influences all of them.

An alternative model of intelligence, due to Godfrey Thomson,[30] a contemporary of Spearman's, suggested that there could be many hidden processes influencing different specific measures of intelligence. Twenty-first-century analyses[31] have found that modern versions of Thomson's theory cannot be distinguished statistically from g theory; in other words, both are equally consistent with the data.

INTELLIGENCE—A MULTIFACETED ENIGMA

So, we have seen that there are lots of ways to think about intelligence in psychology, many ideas about what intelligence is and what it might be useful for, but a lack of broad consensus.

One view, to me, too narrow, is that there is, at root, one kind of intelligence—the type that is measured by IQ tests—and that this underlies and supports everything else. In this view, if AI can capture this fundamental problem-solving ability, then it could apply it to solve all sorts of challenges that we normally consider as requiring human intelligence.

Another point of view is that intelligence tests measure just one facet of human intelligence and that what matters more broadly is not our ability to solve certain kinds of puzzles but our capacity to perform successfully in the real world in terms of the day-to-day skills and abilities that allow us to survive and thrive. According to this view, emotional and social intelligence may be more critical than the logico-mathematical variety when it comes to succeeding in our highly complex social worlds.

A related view would emphasise that different kinds of intelligence underlie the wide range of human talents, and that specialised intelligences allow the most exceptional to display dazzling skill. These include the intelligences underlying creativity in music and art, or the physical intelligence on display in sports, acrobatics, or dance. These different kinds of intelligence might have some overlap, being pieced together of many different component abilities, but every different shade of intelligence may be a different mix. If this *multiple intelligences* view is correct, then AI may progress at different speeds in different domains of intelligence rather than taking broad strides with each advance towards a machine version of general intelligence.

How are we to distinguish between these approaches when, as we have noted, such widely disparate views can each potentially account for much of the evidence from intelligence testing?

Differential psychology, which we have been exploring here, is a form of behavioural science that seeks to understand people by looking at what they do, for example, their performance on intelligence tests. But psychology, and more broadly cognitive science, has other tools up its sleeves. One is *neuroscience*. If we can only get a partial understanding of human intelligence by looking at behaviour, we can add to this by examining the substrates in which it arises; that is, in our bodies and, particularly, in our central nervous systems and brains. We will explore this next in Chapter 3.

Another important approach is *theoretical* psychology, which looks to understand how the mind works at a *functional* level. In other words, it tries to build theories that decompose the mind into different parts, explain how each part operates, and how they come together to create the whole. Theoretical psychology is informed by both the science of human behaviour and by neuroscience and seeks to build on insights generated by both sources of evidence. Theories of mind are, inevitably, very complex. Therefore, they are often systematised and tested using *computer modelling*, just as we use computer models to understand other complex systems, such as the weather and the economy. We can evaluate these models by testing their ability to explain and predict human behaviour, and by their consistency with our understanding of how brains work. We will explore some of these theories of the mind, instantiated as computer models, in later chapters of this book.

For now, maybe we can agree that we have learned something about the nature of intelligence by looking at both the science of human intelligence and some initial efforts to replicate it in AI, but there is still much more to discover.

ADDENDUM

In case you are still puzzled by the question about Peter's age, here is how to get the answer. Peter, who is 12, is three times his brother's age, so his brother must be 4 years old. We can now write the equation $12 + x = 2(4 + x)$ to show that we are trying to calculate the age, $12 + x$, at which Peter is twice his brother's age, 2 times $(4 + x)$. The insight here is that both brothers must age at the same rate, so x, even though we do not know its actual value yet, must be the same on both sides. In computer science terms, x is described as a *variable*. Now we can expand our equation to give $12 + x = 8 + 2x$, re-arrange ($2x-x = 12-8$) and simplify to get $x = 4$. So, Peter will be $12 + 4 = 16$ years old when he is twice the age of his brother, who will then be 8.

If you solved this puzzle, then it is possible you went through some process like this in your head. Another possibility is that rather than solving this equation directly, you worked through the different possible values of x, starting from 1 and increasing by $+1$ each time until you found one that worked (the two sides of the equation balanced). Both strategies are examples of computational thinking. We will look more at the building blocks of natural and artificial thought in Chapter 4.

NOTES

1 Freidenberg, J. (2010). *Artificial Psychology*. London: Psychology Press.
2 Franklin, S. (1995). *Artificial Minds*. Cambridge, MA: MIT Press, and Valentino Braitenberg, V. (1986). *Vehicles: Experiments in Synthetic Psychology*. Cambridge, MA: MIT Press.
3 For a history of automata, see Kang, M. (2011). *Sublime Dreams of Living Machines: The Automaton in the European Imagination*. Cambridge, MA: Harvard University Press. Also look at https://themadmuseum.co.uk/history-of-automata/
4 Hollings, C., Martin, U., & Rice, A. (2018). Ada Lovelace and the analytical engine. Retrieved from https://blogs.bodleian.ox.ac.uk/adalovelace/2018/07/26/ada-lovelace-and-the-analytical-engine/

5 Wiener, N. (1948/1965). *Cybernetics: Or Control and Communication in the Animal and the Machine*. Cambridge, MA: MIT Press.

6 Ashby, W. R. (1952). *Design for a Brain: The Origin of Adaptive Behaviour*. London: Chapman and Hall.

7 McCarthy, J. et al. (1956). *A Proposal for the Dartmouth Summer School Research Project on Artificial Intelligence*. Retrieved from http://jmc.stanford.edu/articles/dartmouth/dartmouth.pdf

8 Simon, H. A. (1960). *The New Science of Management Decision*. New York: Harper & Row. Quote on p. 38.

9 Quoted in Darrach, B. (1970). Meet Shakey the first artificial person. *Life Magazine*, 20th November 1970, 58–68, p. 58c.

10 Ibid, p. 68.

11 Turing, A. M. (1950). Computing machinery and intelligence. *Mind*, 59(236), 433–460.

12 Searle, J. (1990). Is the brain's mind a computer program? *Scientific American*, 262(1), 20–25. For some possible replies, see Churchland, P. M., & Churchland, P. S. (1990). Could a machine think? *Scientific American*, 262(1), 26–31.

13 Ibid, p. 27.

14 Aristotle. (350 BCE). *De Anima* (On the soul), (J. A. Smith, Trans.). Retrieved from https://classics.mit.edu/Aristotle/soul.1.i.html

15 Descartes, R. (1641/1984). *Meditations 1 & 2* (J. Cottingham, Trans.). Boulder: University of Colorado. Retrieved from https://rintintin.colorado.edu/~vancecd/phil201/Meditations.pdf

16 See SkySports. (2011). Testing Ronaldo to the limits. Retrieved from https://youtu.be/z3tnhgGzAs0?si=8zMnp2EkvnZydwje.

17 Binet, A., & Simon, T. (1911). *A Method of Measuring the Development of the Intelligence of Young Children*. Lincoln, IL: Courier Company.

18 Ibid.

19 Gould, S. J. (2006). *The Mismeasure of Man (Revised and Expanded)*. New York: W. W. Norton & Company.

20 Hernstein, R., & Murray, C. (1994). *The Bell Curve: Intelligence and Class Structure in American Life*. Glencoe, IL: Free Press.

21 Wechsler, D. (1958). *The Measurement and Appraisal of Adult Intelligence*. Baltimore, MD: Williams & Wilkins Co.

22 Sternberg, R. J. (1985). *Beyond IQ: A Triarchic Theory of Intelligence*. Cambridge: Cambridge University Press.

23 Gardner, H. (2006). *Multiple Intelligences: New Horizons*. New York: Basic Books.

24 Thorndike, E. L. (1920). Intelligence and its uses. *Harper's Magazine*, 1st January 1920.

25 Salovey, P., & Mayer, J. D. (1990). Emotional intelligence. *Imagination, Cognition & Personality*, 9, 185–211.

26 Damasio, A. R. (1994). *Descartes Error: Emotion, Reason and the Human Brain*. New York: Random House.

27 Goleman, D. (1995). *Emotional Intelligence: Why It Can Matter More Than IQ*. New York: Bantam Books.

28 Kahneman, D. (2011). *Thinking Fast and Slow*. New York: Penguin Books.

29 Spearman, C. (1904). "General intelligence," objectively determined and measured. *The American Journal of Psychology*, 15, 201–292.

30 Thomson, G. H. (1916). A hierarchy without a general factor. *British Journal of Psychology*, 8, 271–281.

31 See review in Conway, A. R. A., & Kovacs, K. (2015). New and emerging models of human intelligence. *Wiley Interdisciplinary Reviews: Cognitive Science*, 6(5), 419–426.

3

BRAINS AND COMPUTERS

PHYSICAL STUFF THAT CAN THINK

When I first saw a slice of human brain in a psychology undergraduate lab class in 1982, I was astonished to think that this slab of strange-looking meat, small enough to hold in my hand, was once part of a structure capable of generating thought. Mind and brain are such very different things it is still hard to conceive that the former must arise in the latter.

Today, we are more familiar with small slabs of physical stuff—smartphones, for example—that can do enormous numbers of complex calculations extremely fast and that support functionality that seems mind-like. For example, the smartphone in your pocket will include an application known as a "personal digital assistant", or PDA, such as *Google Assistant* or *Siri*. You can speak to your PDA, and it will answer questions and give advice. For instance, right now, I can ask Siri to find a local grocery store and then guide me to get there. It is remarkable how quickly we have become accustomed to having handheld devices that can do such things, and it is easy to overlook just how much is involved in resolving this kind of query. Let us explore this a little.

To help with my grocery shopping, my phone, aided by computer servers in the cloud, must first translate a recording of my voice into text, a task that engineers call *speech recognition*. The assistant

DOI: 10.4324/9781003088660-3

must then convert this text—a string of words in whatever language I am speaking—into a machine-intelligible query. This means it must translate my language into a more precise computer code that specifies exactly what it is I want to know or am trying to do. In broad terms, this involves a challenge called *natural language processing* and can involve powerful *search* algorithms to identify material that matches my query. If I ask the PDA to find a nearby shop and take me there, the PDA and the suite of software systems it can command must "know" enough about grocery stores, as places that retail certain kinds of produce, and "understand" sufficiently that I am seeking to visit one.

I have put the words "know" and "understand" in quotes here since, as we saw in Chapter 2, some philosophers consider that machines can never know or understand anything. We will come back to this in Chapter 6, where we will explore what cognitive scientists call the *grounding* problem. For now, let us treat this as a more practical matter.

To give useful advice, the PDA must, for example, be able to distinguish stores from private homes and grocery shops from book shops, hardware shops, and so on. The phone must then be able to access a map, locate me and possible grocery stores on that map, and work out which stores are closest and what would be a suitable and efficient route, depending on my mode of transport. Finally, the device must track my position moment-by-moment, including my orientation, and work out when to give navigation advice, providing verbal and visual prompts in a timely way to guide me to my destination. The spoken language part will involve generating natural language expressions and performing text-to-speech conversion.

Some of these tasks are easier than others; for instance, the PDA can access an online database that will store information about shops and what they sell. The phone can use GPS (Global Positioning System) and wireless signals to find my location, and it will apply a route-finding algorithm to work out and guide me along my route. Decoding speech from different speakers in multiple languages was seen as a comparatively hard problem until relatively recently. However, with advances in neural network technology, machines are now close to human-level ability and, in some ways, better in that they now recognise dozens of languages. Understanding language, that is, accessing the meaning of what someone has said, is a much broader challenge than simply recognising words. However, PDAs are increasingly able to recognise and make sense of a very large range of queries. Recent advances using *large language models* have provided a further significant advance towards generating meaningful text and supporting human-like verbal interaction, as we will explore in Chapter 5.

I have talked here about stores, maps, locations, and language. These are all concepts that mean something to you and me. On your phone, these are all data, which in absolute terms means patterns of numbers, ultimately of binary ones and zeros. This is the universal *digital* code that (nearly) all computers rely on. Computer scientists often talk about *symbols* as patterns of numbers that can stand for or represent something. For example, the letter "A" is often represented as the number 65, which can be written in binary code as 01000001. If you are reading this book in electronic form, then a computer program is processing a document file and sending instructions to create a visual representation of the letter "A" on your screen every time it sees this pattern of bits in the text part of the file.

Manipulating numbers or symbols according to rules or instructions is what computer scientists call *computation* and gives rise to all the reliable and useful behaviours of your smart device. The simplest computations that a computer can do include arithmetic calculations, comparing numbers, writing numbers to memory, and moving numbers from one memory location to another. Complex computations involve putting together millions, billions, or trillions of these basic operations according to a precise procedure specified in a computer program.

To perform computation and to support all these different useful functions for their users, smartphones use many kinds of physical hardware. These include displays, batteries, cameras, microphones, speakers, and so on. Importantly, at the heart of every smart device is a *central processing unit* or CPU—the "brain" of the device, if you will. My iPhone 12 contains the Apple A14 chip. The A14 has six cores (processors), which means that it can run six different programs simultaneously. Each core contains memory, logic, and control units. A key building block is the transistor, a minuscule device made of semiconductor material that allows it to be in one of two states—on or off, one or zero. CPUs such as the A14 are composed of billions of transistors; indeed, the A14 has 11.8 billion transistors, all in a device that fits inside your pocket. This allows your phone to perform computation at a prodigious rate of trillions of instructions per second.

A chip like the A14 comes with an instruction set which includes several hundred basic operations. However, developers do not create apps by using these instructions directly, rather, they use high-level programming languages, like JavaScript, Swift, and Python, in which programs can be specified much more concisely. In any one of these languages, programs are constructed hierarchically. That is, big problems are solved by breaking them into smaller chunks called procedures or functions, which are then broken down into even smaller chunks and ultimately into elementary statements in that language. The step of making this program run inside your phone is called compilation and involves taking all the high-level code and translating it into sequences of instructions described using only the instruction set of the processor. For a computer program that runs on your smartphone, this is the executable file, or app, that sits in your phone's memory and launches when you tap on its icon.

Back in 1982, these technologies, and consumer electronics generally, were in their infancy. The 1970s saw the appearance of the first personal computers and electronic calculators. By the late eighties, programmable computers were getting small enough to be handheld. The first public internet systems appeared at the end of the 1980s, wireless internet (wi-fi) at the end of the 1990s, and data services for phones from around the turn of the millennium. The first commercial speech recognition systems were released in the late 1980s, and the first smartphones in the mid-1990s. The first voice-enabled search app was released by Google as recently as 2010, reflecting the relatively slow emergence of accurate speech recognition in multiple languages. GPS systems for satellite navigation became available for public use in the 1980s, though navigation apps for phones were not launched until the mid-2000s. The first digital personal assistant, Apple's Siri, was launched in 2011, shortly after Google's voice-enabled search.

So, in the pre-mobile days of 1982, I would have needed to find a human being to guide me to the nearest grocery store, particularly someone with local knowledge who spoke my language. Today, I can do all this with just my smartphone via a PDA. You might think that the phone and the servers it relies on are "just" computers running programs, but we should recognise that this set of abilities can be considered a form of AI. Your smartphone is doing tasks that, up until very recently, only humans, with our relatively large biological brains, could do. Let us grant that this is artificial intelligence—is this alien AI, or is what the phone is doing similar to what happens inside human heads? In the rest of this chapter, we will try to shed some light on this question.

A BRIEF DESCRIPTION OF THE BRAIN

The brain, like every other organ in the human body, is made up of billions of small parts in the form of cells. As we have already noted, the cells in the brain that are most important for generating behaviour are called neurons. These are specialised forms of cells that have evolved for processing and communication within the body, but in other ways, they are like every other cell in the body. For instance, they have a nucleus which carries genetic material, various internal organelles such as those that convert food into energy, and a cell membrane which limits what can pass in and out.

The average human brain has around *one hundred billion* neurons and many more non-neural cells. A key difference between neurons and other cells is that neurons emit thousands of projections, like the roots of a plant, that they use to communicate with other neurons and with sensory and motor cells throughout the body (see the central panel of Figure 2.2). Specifically, neurons send out long threads, called *dendrites*, that connect to other neurons at special junctions called *synapses*. Neurons also transmit their own signals to communicate with others along another special thin tube called the *axon*. A typical cell in your forebrain has between ten and thirty thousand synaptic connections, so the human brain, or the human *connectome* as it is sometimes described, therefore, has trillions of connections, perhaps as many as *one hundred trillion*.

Neurons work by passing signals in bursts of brief electrical pulses known as *spikes*. Spikes have something of an all-or-nothing quality; that is, a neuron is either generating spikes or it is quiet. The spikes that run along the axon affect the neurons that they connect to via the intervening synapses, making the cell on the other side of each synapse more or less likely to fire. Activity at a synapse that increases the likelihood that the next neuron will fire is called *excitatory*, while activity that reduces that likelihood is called *inhibitory*.

Individual neurons are generally either excitatory or inhibitory depending on what type of synapse they form, so brains can be thought of as vast networks of neurons in which patterns of activity can spread like wildfire through excitatory connections, or they can be damped and extinguished by the action of inhibitory neurons. The firing patterns of large populations of neurons can become synchronised, leading to peaks and troughs in the electrical activity of the brain that can be described as wave-like *oscillations*. When you are sleeping, your cortical neurons become widely synchronised and oscillate at around 1 Hz, that is, one cycle per second. However, in the awake brain, oscillations happen at multiple higher frequencies of up to 100 Hz and beyond. For example, oscillations between 13 and 30 Hz become prominent when you are actively engaged in problem-solving. One popular theory is that this synchronisation of neural firing helps to create coherence in the vast and distributed patterns of neural firing that we find in awake brains.

I have mentioned that neurons are either firing or quiet. This somewhat resembles the electronic transistors we looked at earlier, which were either on or off—one or zero. This resemblance of neurons to digital devices led the neuroscientist Warren McCulloch and his mathematician colleague, Walter Pitts, to propose, in a paper published in 1943,[1] that neurons, like computers, could carry out certain kinds of logical operations.

Nevertheless, it would be wrong to describe neurons as simply digital devices. Yes, a neuron is either firing or not firing; however, the temporal patterning of spikes along the axon, the effects of neurochemicals on the behaviour of the cell, and the general biological complexity of cells suggest that there is a great deal more going on, some of which we do not understand yet.

Let us think about the timing of neural firing first. Some neurons fire in regular and repeated patterns in response to input, sometimes with the rate of firing proportional to stimulus intensity. This kind of behaviour is relatively easy to understand. However, other neurons fire in bursts of multiple spikes, followed by pauses, whilst others may produce intermittent spikes that are unpredictable and may even be random.

Alongside the electrical activity carried along the axons and dendrites, neurons also communicate chemically through compounds called *neurotransmitters* and *neuromodulators*. Indeed, most synapses work by converting the electrical signal on the presynaptic side of the junction into a chemical messenger. The chemical then crosses the gap to the other side of the synapse, where it triggers a further electrical response. The chemicals that are involved in synaptic transmission are called neurotransmitters.

Neuromodulators are chemicals that have a more diffuse role. They can be released by neurons or carried in the bloodstream like hormones, and their effects can last from a few milliseconds to minutes. There are many neuromodulators, including several that you may have heard of, such as *norepinephrine* (also called noradrenaline) and *oxytocin*. For instance, norepinephrine, which is released when we are fearful or stressed, helps prepare the brain and body for vigorous activity such as fighting or running away. Oxytocin, which is released when people touch each other in a gentle way, helps to create emotional bonds, such as that between parent and child, and is involved in social behaviour and emotional regulation.

Some neurochemicals can function as both neurotransmitters (locally released in synapses) and as neuromodulators (diffusing through the brain). *Dopamine*, for instance, plays a vital role in signalling when something unexpectedly good has happened and is important for learning. *Serotonin* has multiple roles and is important in regulating mood and sleep. Although an important neurotransmitter, most of the serotonin in your body comes from cells lining your intestines and travels to the brain via your blood. This is one of the many ways in which parts of the body that are not your nervous system influence how you think. Many medications for mood disorders such as anxiety and depression operate to increase the levels of serotonin in the brain.

The effects of these brain chemicals are more *analogue*, meaning graded or continuous, rather than *digital* (on or off). So overall, we should think of neurons not as analogue or digital devices but as a hybrid with properties of both. Moreover, neurons are undoubtedly more complex than transistors, but we might still usefully think of them as *processors*, that is, as devices that can store memory and make decisions based on their previous state and pattern of inputs. Note that a processor is not necessarily a digital device. Indeed, technologies such as the wristwatch and the slide rule can be thought of as *analogue processors* (or computers) that use continuously varying physical signals to keep time or to calculate.

Today, the field of *computational neuroscience*,[2] founded by McCulloch and Pitts, creates mathematical models of single neurons considered as complex processors—part digital, part analogue. In a typical model, a simulated neuron takes inputs from other model cells, modifies these according to the excitatory or inhibitory nature of the intervening synapses, and generates an output that is a sequence of synthetic spikes. All of this can be described using mathematical equations that can be simulated on a digital computer, including the effects of neuromodulators, which can be included as additional parameters or by defining further equations that approximate how these chemicals diffuse through the brain. Many different neuron types can now be simulated with a high level of precision.

Just as we can simulate single neurons, computational neuroscientists can also simulate networks of neurons, and ultimately, we could imagine simulating entire brains. In 2023, the HPE Frontier supercomputer can do one million trillion floating point operations per second,[3] more than enough to simulate the one hundred trillion connections in the human brain if we knew how to write that program.

Computing chips are also being developed that are more directly inspired by how biological neurons operate and interact, leading to more brain-inspired forms of artificial computation. For instance, the A14 chip in my iPhone already includes a 16-core "neural engine" that is optimised for tasks that require parallel processing, such as image analysis, motion detection, and natural language understanding. In what follows, and in Chapter 5, we will explore why these kinds of tasks often involve brain-like computation. Intel's prototype neuromorphic Loihi chip has other brain-like properties, including the capacity to model 130,000 active neurons with up to 1,000 synapses per neuron. These artificial neurons communicate asynchronously using signals resembling neural spikes.

BRAINS AS COMPUTATIONAL SYSTEMS

An open question is whether a simulated brain would be capable of thought in the same way as a biological brain. Of course, we are never going to simulate all the biological details of what is happening in neurons and brains, but how close do we need to get to create an artificial system that can think?

Using computer models, we can simulate weather systems with increasing accuracy and precision. However, no one imagines that a simulated rainstorm could ever make you wet. In the same way, a simulation of the brain is never going to have any of the physical properties of brain chemistry.

Why, then, does anyone think that the brain is different from the weather? A core hypothesis of modern cognitive science is that the *brain is fundamentally a computational system*; that is, it performs operations on data according to rules.

The types of computation the brain performs resemble what mathematicians would describe as statistical operations over large datasets that have significant intrinsic noise. They are, therefore, rather different from the strictly logical and noise-free operations of conventional computers. This has led some scientists and philosophers to argue that brains are not like computers. However, AI is increasingly relying on noisier statistical algorithms to solve the most difficult AI problems. The computing programs that do this are called *artificial neural networks* due to their obvious inspiration from the networks of biological neurons we find in brains. We will explore these in some detail in Chapter 5. Running on neuromorphic hardware, these AIs increasingly look as though they are performing the kinds of computation we see in brains.

Does it matter if simulated brains lack physical neurons, synapses, or neuromodulators?

Possibly not, according to a hypothesis that cognitive scientists have been investigating since at least the invention of computers that goes by the name of *functionalism*. The key idea is that it matters not so much what brains and computers are made of—they are undoubtedly made of very different kinds of stuff—but what they do, that is, their *function*.

An early insight that supports functionalism was provided by Alan Turing[4] who showed that any device that can compute with numerical data can, in principle, emulate any other. This means that we could build computers out of string and sealing wax if we wished (of course, this is not practical, hence the "in principle"). This also means that a sufficiently powerful modern digital computer, such as the HPE Frontier, has the potential to mimic a biological hybrid, such as the brain.

FROM BRAINS TO MINDS

We have seen that brains are networks of biological cells that are highly interconnected and influence each other by electrical and chemical signalling, but how does this system give rise to intelligence?

Although individual neurons are complex cells, few people would want to argue that neurons are individually intelligent. Instead, intelligence happens when we have a sufficiently large network of neurons to make up a brain—as Marvin Minsky once said, "the mind is made up of things that are mindless".[5] Moreover, to display intelligence and to configure itself in the first place, the brain must be appropriately connected to other parts of the body—eyes, ears, limbs, and muscles—such that it can sense and act. We will look further at the role of the body in intelligence in Chapter 6, where we will consider forms of embodied AI such as robots. For now, we will focus on the brain itself, how it is composed of different kinds of neurons and neural networks, and how those come together to make a functioning system that is capable (with the body) of acting, thinking, and experiencing.

The problem of building brains out of brain cells is a problem of *architecture*. Architecture means largely the same thing whether we are talking about buildings or brains. A cathedral has a certain structure, function, and appearance because of how the different materials that compose that building have been put together according to a precise and carefully crafted plan. The brain is no different, except that the plan, which has been devised through evolution, is completely unknown to us. Like an archaeologist discovering a building created by some lost civilisation, we can try to uncover the plan by examining the structure we have discovered. Unlike a building, though, which is largely a stationary structure, and where appearance is a good guide to purpose, brains are continuously changing, active structures, and their appearance—large puffball-like lumps of squidgy tissue—gives few clues to function.

With billions of component parts, trying to understand the brain at the cellular level is going to be extremely challenging, likely impossible. Instead, the approach we should follow is to think of the brain at multiple scales—from neurons to networks, and from there to networks of networks that connect the different parts of the brain and link the brain with the body.

Understanding the functional architecture of the brain is one of the biggest challenges facing science today, but there is a lot we already know. Here, I will summarise some key ideas that will be useful later in this book.

NEURONS, NETWORKS, MAPS, AND MICROCIRCUITS

Let us start with neurons. As we have seen, there is more than one kind of neuron, indeed, there are several hundred, possibly thousands of different neuron types in the human brain. When we think about what the different parts of the brain are doing, it will be important to understand which different types of neurons are involved and how they individually and collectively contribute to the overall pattern of activity. Neurons may signal in different ways, as previously discussed, such as through regular spikes or bursts. They may have their effect by releasing neuromodulators or by triggering muscle fibres. In some situations, a single spike from one neuron may carry important information. More often, a pattern of firing across thousands or millions of neurons will be needed to trigger a decision or an action.

For example, lining the back of your eyeball, there is a sensory sheet called the retina that we can think of as an extension of the brain. The retina has over sixty different types of neurons that differ in shape, size, neurochemistry, and, importantly, sensitivity to different kinds of light. The cells that respond directly to light entering the eye are the rod and cone cells. The rod cells, of which there are around 120 million, are sensitive to brightness whilst the six million cone cells respond to different wavelengths of light and hence colour—typically red, yellow/green, and blue. On the output side of the retina, there are around 1.2 million retinal ganglion cells, so significant compression, at a ratio of around 10:1, and other forms of preprocessing are already happening between the light-sensitive neurons and this output layer. Besides brightness and colour, these output cells signal other attributes of the visual image, including contrast, motion, flicker, and texture. By comparison, a modern smartphone will have at least a 12-million-pixel array (so around 1/10th the resolution of the eye) built from a special kind of light-sensitive transistor. In RAW format, each pixel is encoded as three numbers, one each for red, green, and blue, with 10–16 bits per number (i.e., between one thousand and sixty-six thousand levels per colour). Digital cameras also use compression; for instance, the popular "jpeg" format compresses images with little loss of detail, again at a ratio of around 10:1.

Although there are many differences between eyes and modern digital cameras, the basic principle of coding light into a vast array of electrical signals is shared. The sensitivity of the retina is impressive—a single photon of light is sufficient to activate a rod cell, though typically, a larger number of photons, arriving around the same time, will be required to register a response in the brain.

What about networks? When we look at the brain under a microscope, even under low magnification, we can see that some parts of the brain are mostly neurons, called *grey matter*, and other parts are mostly connective tissue, called *white matter*. There are also some fluid-filled spaces called *ventricles*. There are many assemblies, called *nuclei*, of highly connected networks of neurons, and there are *layered* structures, as we have already encountered with the six-layer structure of the cerebral cortex.

The patterns of connectivity between neurons throughout the brain are highly organised. Most neurons have most of their connections with neighbouring cells, but some will have long-range connections, such as those in the motor part of the cortex whose axons reach down into the spinal cord, where they control the fine movements of your limbs and digits.

There are also important regularities that give strong clues about function. For example, the neurons in the retina are laid out in two-dimensional sheets so that neighbouring cells capture light from nearby parts of the environment. This pattern is preserved as signals travel through the pathways of the visual brain. The density of photoreceptive cells varies across the retina, with the highest concentration at the sensory *fovea*, in the centre of the visual field, reducing by a factor of fifty or so towards the periphery. Similarly, areas of skin are mapped to networks of touch cells in the tactile brain that also preserve spatial layout but distort spatial size. So, for instance, the sensory areas of the brain corresponding to the highly sensitive fingertips and lips are much more extensive than those for large areas of relatively unresponsive skin, such as in the middle of your back. This indicates that the brain is devoting a lot more resources to understanding what is happening in the skin areas we typically use to explore our world.

This geometric layout of the brain, using *maps* that preserve adjacency, is a way of reducing connection costs and improving energy efficiency. It is also a way of coding information about the spatial layout of the body and the world without having to do so explicitly, letting geometry do some of the computational work.

In many regions of the brain, we see what appear to be *microcircuits* that are replicated over and over again millions of times. For instance, in the cortex, we find circuits of neurons with predictable patterns of organisation that connect vertically across all six layers— corresponding to around 3mm in depth (yes, it is that thin!)—but within a local horizontal region less than half a millimetre in diameter (see Figure 2.2, right). In 1957, the neuroscientist Vernon Mountcastle[6] proposed that these cortical *columns*, each containing something like ten thousand neurons, form modular processors that make a similar contribution to function wherever they are found. One popular theory is that the *cortical microcircuit* is configured to *predict its own inputs*. As we will see in Chapters 5 and 6, AI research has shown that processors with this capability could be a useful building block whether you are trying to understand the world through sensing, generating spoken language, or acting in the world through movement.

Another type of microcircuit exists at the back of the brain in a structure called the *cerebellum* (the "little brain" in Latin). Although originally thought to be involved in controlling movement, the cerebellum, which contains more than half of all the neurons in the entire brain, is now known to be involved in many different functions. These range from movement and balance to speech and language, sensory processing, and social behaviour. Like the cortex, the cerebellum contributes a similar component of functionality to all these different capacities. Specifically, the *cerebellar microcircuit* seems to be good for tuning up other systems in the brain to be more accurate, for instance, it helps us to articulate speech, precisely time actions, and so on.

LEARNING

When we are born, nearly all the neurons in our brains are already present. But something important happens in the first few months of infancy and continues for the rest of our lives—the connections between neurons grow and change. In particular, the strength of transmission at synapses changes, sometimes very quickly. Many of these changes are in response to experience and, therefore, constitute forms of *learning*. A key finding is that the different parts of the brain seem to do different kinds of learning.

For example, the cortex learns to find patterns in complex signals, such as the continuous stream of spikes relaying information about colour, and areas of light and dark, from your eyes. Somehow the cortex learns to make sense of these signals so that it can recognise objects, places, familiar faces, and so on. Because this part of the brain seems to learn without a teacher—perhaps, as noted earlier, by predicting its own inputs—this kind of learning is called *unsupervised*.

The cerebellum, on the other hand, seems to be involved in another kind of learning that relies on training signals coming from elsewhere in the brain. Because this learning involves an external teaching signal it is called *supervised*.

A third area of the brain, called the *basal ganglia*, a group of structures that lie beneath the cortex, seems to be specialised to learn from intermittent training signals, that indicate when something unexpectedly good or bad has happened. This is usually described as a form of *reinforcement* learning. There is a training signal, but it is non-specific; it does not tell you where you went right or wrong but only whether the outcome was better or worse than expected. This kind of learning signal can originate from the environment, for instance, when you find food or when someone you care about applauds or reproaches you.

We will explore some aspects of learning in AIs and in brains in more detail in Chapter 5.

PRINCIPLES OF BRAIN ARCHITECTURE

The huge number of different structures and local networks in the brain is confusing even for expert neuroscientists. Are there any general principles that might help us understand what is happening across the entire brain? Yes, here we will explore just a few.

The first principle is *modularity*. A functional system, such as the brain, is modular to the extent that it can be divided into separable sub-systems that make different contributions. Most human-engineered systems are highly modular. Think of a car. It is made up of thousands of distinct parts that are organised into sub-systems— engine, gearbox, cooling, transmission, etc. The human body is also highly modular; for instance, we have separate systems for respiration, circulation, digestion, vision, audition, and, of course, the nervous system. The nervous system divides into the central nervous system— the brain and spinal cord—and the peripheral nervous system that interfaces with the body. But does the brain also have sub-systems? Indeed, it does. We have already encountered an example of modularity in the distinct columns of the cerebral cortex. In Chapter 2, I also noted that there is a more global specialisation. For instance, sensory areas, such as the *visual cortex*, are located towards the back of the brain, while areas that are more involved in motor control are clustered towards the front. Within these different cortical regions, we see further evidence of modularity. For instance, within the visual parts of the cortex, there are regions dedicated to processing different aspects of vision such as colour, position, depth, movement, and so on. Within the auditory cortex, there are sub-areas that are responsive to sounds at different wavelengths, including ones that are specialised for detecting speech sounds. In contrast, nearer to those parts of the motor cortex that correspond to the face, we find regions that are specialised in generating human language, such as a zone in the left frontal lobe called *Broca's area*. Damage to this area typically leaves language understanding intact but causes difficulties in producing fluent and grammatically correct speech.

Modularity in the cortex has been estimated by examining the anatomical connectivity of different parts of the brain—literally, which parts connect to which, and functional connectivity—which parts are active at the same time and sharing information during specific tasks. Both approaches demonstrate that the cortex is modular in multiple ways and at different scales.[7] For example, anatomical analyses have found that the cortex can be divided into four general sub-systems for vision, hearing, body sensing and motor control, and planning and motivation. Other functional analyses have identified a *default mode* network of structures and pathways that are active when the brain is not directly involved in any specific task. This network may be important for remembering the past or thinking about the future.

Elsewhere in the brain, modularity is even more evident. I have already mentioned the specialised circuitry of the cerebellum, which makes a similar contribution to all the different functional sub-systems in which it operates. Another highly specialised structure is the *medulla*, a stem-like extension of the spinal cord, which contains local circuits that are critical for many physiological functions, including heartbeat, blood pressure, and breathing.

A further example is the *suprachiasmatic nucleus* located at the base of the brain. This nucleus provides you with your "body clock" and is important in generating and maintaining the circadian rhythm, which underlies the sleep/wake cycle. People who have damage to this part of the brain, for instance, as the result of a stroke or brain tumour, may struggle to maintain a 24-hour daily pattern and often have periods of alertness and sleepiness at irregular times during the day.

Note that modularity in the brain is less straightforward than it is in human-engineered systems. For instance, motor areas can play a role in sensory processing and vice versa—as we noted in Chapter 2, there is no neat division between sensing and thinking (intellect). At any time, most of your brain is active in some way or another, suggesting a highly distributed system. However, different parts and sub-systems are clearly making quite different contributions to the overall functioning of the brain at any moment. This balance between locally modular and globally distributed processing is one of the key puzzles that brain scientists have begun to unlock in recent decades, overcoming historical views that over-emphasised either modular or distributed processing alone. Evidence of modularity can be seen as support for the idea of multiple intelligences discussed in Chapter 2.

A second principle is *layering*. We have already encountered layered networks in the cortex, but the brain is also a layered structure at a coarser scale. Specifically, you may know that the brain roughly divides into a *hindbrain*, a *midbrain*, and a *forebrain*, which includes the cortex (see Figure 2.2, left). Across these three different layers, which are found in all vertebrate animals, there are similarities in function across all three levels.[8] That is, for common activities that animals engage in, we find structures in the hindbrain, midbrain, and forebrain that are involved in regulating them. Typically, pathways through the hindbrain are fast, rely on sensory signals that are relatively unprocessed, and generate immediate, sometimes reflexive responses. Those in the midbrain tend to involve a greater degree of sensory analysis, and the behaviours they command are often more complex, but they are also often innate; that is, we are largely born with these capacities. Finally, the forebrain is the slowest to wire up in development, performs the most complex analyses of the sensory world, and generates the most complex responses, often as a result of learning.

Where related but complementary functionalities are layered one on top of the other, this architecture makes brains very robust—if one sub-system breaks down, there is often another way to solve the problem. However, the higher-level systems typically rely on the lower-level ones to work, but not vice versa. That is, you could still function without parts of your forebrain, but the hindbrain, which, as we have seen, is involved in regulating many of the core functions of the body, such as breathing and heartbeat, is an essential interface and control system for the rest of the body. Damage to critical parts of the hindbrain will result in an early death.

A third principle is that brains exploit *attractor dynamics*, an idea that comes from the physics of complex dynamical systems.[9] A complex system is one that has multiple interacting parts, and a dynamical system is simply one that changes over time. Our solar system is a complex dynamical system—the planets and the sun being the parts and their interaction being due to the force of gravity. Our brains are another such system, the billions of neurons being the parts and their interactions being due to their synaptic connections, neuromodulation, and so on.

The science of complex dynamical systems, or *systems science* for short, shows that complex dynamical systems tend to have preferred states that they visit over and over. For instance, the planets in our solar system have their orbits. These preferred states are called "attractors" because the system will tend towards such a pattern when starting from a random state and will move back towards such a pattern if diverted away. Your brain will also have preferred states. That is, out of all the countless ways in which the neurons of the brain could interact to produce patterns of activity, some patterns will be strongly preferred over others. Attractor dynamics helps explain how a massively distributed system such as the brain can produce coherent behaviour across all its parts and how such a system can rapidly flip from one attractor, or behaviour pattern, to another when something changes, for instance, when some new sensory input arrives.

One final principle is what I will call *centralised action selection*. Although the networks of the brain may be finely tuned to exploit attractor dynamics, there appear to be important benefits in having some more centralised forms of coordination that guarantee that your brain does not try to do two incompatible things at the same time.

Along the central line of the brain, we find a group of structures that seems to be specialised for exactly that.[10] These include a group of mid- and forebrain structures called the *basal ganglia*, which, as we have already noted, are an important site for learning. The basal ganglia appear to hold a veto over all voluntary movement (that is, movement that is not a reflex response to a stimulus). This means that before any part of the brain can command an action, it needs to send signals to the basal ganglia, and these structures then need to remove inhibition from the motor system to allow the body to act. Similar pathways operate internally so that the basal ganglia can also gate cognitive operations (such as thinking) elsewhere in the brain. When this system is badly damaged, for instance, in late-stage *Parkinson's disease*, people can lose the ability to generate voluntary action. If you suffer from this debilitating ailment, you might will yourself to move but simply be unable to command your muscles to respond.

Whilst attractor dynamics plays a powerful role in determining how the brain responds to the world, one reason that the brain may have evolved these centralised systems is the importance of making fast and appropriate decisions about what to do next. Animals that were slow or indecisive would be at a big disadvantage, for instance, in evading predators, compared to ones that had evolved fast, specialised systems for cleanly selecting actions. Act quickly, or get eaten!

The role of learning in the basal ganglia means that action selection can also improve through experience. If an action selected by the basal ganglia leads to an unexpected reward, then learning can adjust the pattern of synaptic connections so that the same action is more likely to be selected next time a similar situation arises. Conversely, if bad things happen, that action can be made less likely next time. This learning process, which uses the neurotransmitter dopamine as a learning signal, seems to be a key substrate for acquiring new skills and habit formation in the human brain.

REPLACING BRAIN PARTS WITH ELECTRONICS

The architecture of the brain, as just described, may seem rather different from anything we find in current-day computers. So, where does this leave us in answering the question of whether AI systems resemble the brain? We will explore these questions in more depth in the following chapters, where we will also see that as we start to build AIs that can act in the world, there is an increasing convergence between the functional principles I have outlined for brains and computational architectures that are proving useful in AI and robotics.

Brains are quite different from computers in how they are configured and the materials they are made of. Nevertheless, there is nothing we have discovered so far about brains that suggests that their component parts, and thus ultimately entire brains, cannot be understood and potentially replicated using artificial computational systems, that is, by computers. One reason to be confident about this is that we are already replacing parts of the nervous system with artificial devices built around specialised computers without external interfaces called *embedded processors*. These devices are working to do the job of the parts they are replacing or to restore the functionality of damaged circuits. To conclude this chapter, I will explore some recent examples.

One device that is already in widespread use for people with loss of hearing is the *cochlear implant*. The cochlea is the part of the inner ear that contains specialised sensory hairs for detecting sounds at different wavelengths. When soundwaves reach these hairs, they bend, creating sensory signals that encode sound as electrical signals that are relayed to different parts of the brain, such as the auditory cortex. The artificial cochlea bypasses a damaged ear by using a microphone, together with a miniature sound processor and an electrode array, to create exactly the right kind of electric signals in the auditory nerve to restore hearing.

Progress is also being made to replace the retina in people who have lost their sight. Again, the idea is to replace the sensory neurons (rod, cone, and ganglion cells) with processors, this time using a tiny camera and creating electrical signals relayed directly to the output side of the retina and from there to the visual brain. Although this technology is less mature than the cochlear implant, there are early-stage devices that are restoring some vision in people who were previously completely blind.

Patients with Parkinson's disease can be fitted with implants that provide a form of stimulation to those parts of the basal ganglia that are malfunctioning due to the disease. When suitably tuned and targeted, this electrical stimulation can correct the circuit to be closer to its normal state, relieving some of the symptoms of Parkinson's, such as tremors and difficulty in initiating movement.

More recently, a research team led by the neuroengineer Henri Lorach[11] has shown that it is possible to bridge across a broken spinal cord by placing embedded processors on either side of the break that communicate wirelessly via Bluetooth. The processor on the brain side of the break encodes commands generated by motor neurons into digital signals that are conveyed to a second processor on the body side of the break, where they are converted back into neural signals that can be used to trigger muscles. One patient who had suffered a life-changing spine injury in a cycling accident was able to walk again and climb stairs. Other labs have used cortical implant technology to allow paralysed patients to control robot arms and hands simply by thinking.

Technologies that are under development in research labs go even further. For example, researchers led by the neuroengineer Simeon Bamford have demonstrated that a microchip programmed with a model of the cerebellar microcircuit could operate in an anaesthetised rat to replicate some of the effects of learning in the cerebellum.[12] The chip received signals from the input side of the cerebellum and injected signals back into the output side of the cerebellum, thus bypassing the biological microcircuit.

Work is underway to see if similar technologies can be developed to bypass microcircuits in the forebrain. Ultimately, these technologies could be used to repair damaged brains and potentially extend the brain, for instance, by allowing digital devices to act as a form of external memory that is directly interfaced to the relevant areas of the biological brain. This work could eventually treat conditions that cause amnesia (catastrophic forgetting), such as *Alzheimer's disease*. It is possible that such an implant could operate so intuitively as to feel like a core component of everyday thought. That is, one day, you could access your electronic memories just by thinking, as you do your biologically encoded ones.

If we can replace one part of the nervous system with an electronic substitute, then it is possible to imagine replacing all its parts. The futurist Hans Moravec has proposed this as a thought experiment.[13] Imagine gradually replacing all the neurons in your brain with their electronic equivalent, perhaps one sub-circuit or cortical column at a time. At what point would you start to feel and think differently? At what point would you transition from being a biological intelligence to an AI? Would the resulting electronic brain still have human-like experience and consciousness?

The ideas we have explored in this chapter suggest that it is possible to conceive of artificial devices that think like brains. In the next chapter, we will delve into some of the fundamental problems that AI can already solve, and the computational building blocks these algorithms use. We will also further explore what this can tell us about the psychology of human intelligence.

NOTES

1 McCulloch, W. S., & Pitts, W. (1943). A logical calculus of the ideas immanent in nervous activity. *The Bulletin of Mathematical Biophysics*, 5(4), 115–133.

2 Sejnowski, T. J., Koch, C., & Churchland, P. S. (1990). Computational neuroscience. In S. J. Hanson & C. R. Olson (Eds.), *Connectionist Modeling and Brain Function the Developing Interface*. Cambridge, MA: MIT Press.

3 See *Time Magazine* "Best inventions of 2023". Retrieved from https://time.com/collection/best-inventions-2023/6325636/hewlett-packard-enterprise-frontier-supercomputer/

4 Turing, A. M. (1936–1937). On computable numbers, with an application to the Entscheidungs problem. *Proceedings of the London Mathematical Society*, s2–42, 230–265.

5 Minsky, M. L. (1986). *The Society of Mind*. New York: Simon & Schuster.

6 Mountcastle, V. B. (1957). Modality and topographic properties of single neurons of cat's somatic sensory cortex. *Journal of Neurophysiology*, 20(4), 408–434.

7 Meunier, D., Lambiotte, R., Fornito, A., Ersche, K., & Bullmore, E. (2009). Hierarchical modularity in human brain functional networks. *Frontiers in Neuroinformatics*, 3.

8 Prescott, T. J., Redgrave, P., & Gurney, K (1999). Layered control architectures in robots and vertebrates. *Adaptive Behavior*, 7(1), 99–127.

9 Kelso, J. A. S. (1995). *Dynamic Patterns: The Self-organization of Brain and Behaviour*. Cambridge, MA: MIT Press.

10 Redgrave, P., Prescott, T. J., & Gurney, K. (1999). The basal ganglia: a vertebrate solution to the selection problem? *Neuroscience*, 89(4), 1009–1023.

11 Lorach, H. et al. (2023). Walking naturally after spinal cord injury using a brain–spine interface. *Nature*, 618(7963), 126–133.

12 Bamford, S. A. et al. (2012). A VLSI field-programmable mixed-signal array to perform neural signal processing and neural modeling in a prosthetic system. *IEEE Transactions on Neural Systems and Rehabilitation Engineering*, 20(4), 455–467.

13 Moravec, H. (1988). *Mind Children: The Future of Robot and Human Intelligence*. Cambridge, MA: Harvard University Press.

4

THE BUILDING BLOCKS OF INTELLIGENCE

DEDUCTIVE REASONING

As a postgraduate student in a course on "applied artificial intelligence" in 1989, one of the first things I learned to do was to manipulate ideas using logic. Being logical is something we associate with computers and artificial intelligence, but it is also a fundamental human skill practised since classical times.

Indeed, Aristotle, whom we have already encountered as a founder of psychology, was in many ways the original cognitive scientist, interested in understanding and formalising the nature of thought by uncovering its principles. Aristotle developed one of the best-known forms of logical reasoning—the *syllogism*. Syllogistic reasoning allows you to start from some statements that you know or assume to be true and then identify some conclusions that must necessarily be true as a consequence. This is an example of what we call *deductive reasoning*.

Aristotle wrote, "A deduction is speech in which, certain things having been supposed, something different from those supposed results of necessity because of their being so".[1] This claim is rather

DOI: 10.4324/9781003088660-4

densely expressed (to say the least); let us unpack it by considering a classic example:

All humans are mortal.
Socrates is a human.
Therefore, Socrates is mortal.

Here, there are two premises, "all humans are mortal" and "Socrates is human", from which we deduce one consequence—"Socrates is mortal". The conclusion is hardly surprising, even to someone who has never thought about logic. Of course, Socrates is mortal; he is human, after all! What the syllogism does is show how this inference can be achieved in a more formal way—one that makes the processes involved more explicit. Specifically, Aristotle showed how you could automatically derive new knowledge ("something different") based on existing knowledge ("certain things") through (logical) "necessity". The form of the syllogism means that you can take the same structure and apply it to different content and know that you will always be able to derive valid conclusions (given valid premises).

Why are the rules of logic true? Well, for Aristotle, it was simply a case of their "being so". You might also argue that logic, like mathematics, must be true because it has turned out to be so useful for understanding the world.

Although a single syllogism might seem so simple as to be hardly worth bothering with, the power of logical thinking comes when we start to chain arguments together. In the case of the syllogism, this is called a polysyllogism. Consider another classic example:

It is raining.
If we go outside while it is raining, we will get wet.
If we get wet, we will get cold.
Therefore, if we go outside, we will get cold.

This can be re-written to show that this argument is just two syllogisms chained together such that the conclusion of the first becomes a premise for the second:

It is raining.
If we go outside while it is raining, we will get wet.
Therefore, if we go outside, we will get wet.

If we go outside, we will get wet.
If we get wet, we will get cold.
Therefore, if we go outside, we will get cold.

One way to think of this is that we are taking a form of common-sense reasoning and expressing it in such a way that all the steps we take to reach a conclusion are made more explicit. People were able to reason deductively before Aristotle and still do without ever having heard of logic.

Of course, you know that if you go out in the rain, you will get wet and that if you get wet, you might get cold. For that reason, the sensible thing is not to go out in the rain or, if you do, to take an umbrella. One proposal is that your mind, without you necessarily knowing it, has reasoned to that conclusion based on a series of inferences not unlike Aristotle's syllogisms (there are other possibilities you may have learned from experience, as we will see in Chapter 5).

A similar deductive inference process has been systematised in the form of AI *expert systems*, also known as *knowledge-based systems*, that use logical structures composed of *if-then* rules that are similar to syllogisms and are also called *production rules*. Like syllogisms, productions can be sequenced together to generate new inferences. Called *forward-chaining*, this establishes new facts based on existing ones that, together with existing facts, fire further rules, and so on. Systems of this type are widely deployed in areas such as customer support, financial services, intelligent tutoring, and medical diagnosis, often behind online chatbots. So, you may well have used this kind of AI without knowing it.

In the 19th century, Aristotelian logic was built on by other thinkers, such as the philosopher Gottlob Frege, who developed a formal language—*predicate logic*—for representing and reasoning about ideas.[2] Frege invented the idea of *variables*, replacing statements such as "Socrates is a human" with the more general form "there exists an x such that x is Socrates and x is human". Predicate logic paved the way for the programming languages we use today. Around the same time, the mathematician George Boole, in a book called *The Laws of Thought*,[3] developed what is today called *symbolic logic* using the shorthand of symbols, such as x and y, in place of natural language expressions to perform deductive reasoning. Statements can then be associated with truth values; that is, they can be identified as either *true* or *false* and then combined with logical operators, such as *and*, *or*, and *not*. All of this can, of course, be expressed with numbers. Indeed, the core duality of logic—truth and falsity—maps neatly onto the binary values of one and zero.

Deduction is such a powerful process that it underlies most of the principles and ideas we have in mathematics. Indeed, nearly all the important ideas in maths have been validated through a process of deductive reasoning, starting with existing principles that had previously been deduced. Gottlob Frege is recognised as formalising this idea of a mathematical "proof". Note, though, this does not mean that all ideas in mathematics originated through deduction. Rather, having arrived at a new insight, a mathematician will generally look to deduction to prove that this new idea is necessarily correct. Indeed, in the age of AI, mathematicians will often use *automated theorem provers* to help establish a formal proof for a mathematical conjecture. We will explore other ways in which ideas can originate through this book while recognising that the processes underlying true originality in thought remain somewhat mysterious!

Another challenge for deduction is that given a few useful pieces of knowledge, we can deduce others; however, most of these deductions might be quite banal and rather useless. For example, if I go outside while it is raining, I can conclude that I will get wet, that my clothes will get wet, that my hair will get wet (if I am not wearing a hat), and so on. This is all very true, but perhaps not helpful. How, in deductive logic, can we prioritise deducing useful conclusions relevant to our goals and needs?

A further issue, termed the *frame problem*, was identified by John McCarthy and his collaborator Patrick Hayes.[4] If something changes in the world, how many of the existing facts that I have already deduced do I need to re-assess? Even more broadly, how can I decide what is worth reasoning about and what is not? This indicates that all thought cannot be just deduction.

INDUCTION AND CAUSALITY

If deduction were the only way to discover anything, then we would be rather limited in what we know. Deduction reveals things that are true on account of other things we already know to be true. In a way, it never tells us anything truly new because, if you were being particularly pedantic, you could argue that once you have the basic set of facts and the rules of logic, then everything else that you could deduce is implicitly known already.

One domain that is concerned with the discovery of a different kind of knowledge is science. Indeed, when we look at science, we see that its core methodology is not deduction, although that certainly has a role, but what we can call induction.

Induction proceeds by observation; we look at the world and see that certain patterns are repeated over and over. For instance, for countless generations, our ancestors have observed that the sun rises in the east and sets in the west. Repeated observations of sunrise and sunset, the cycles of movement of the moon, the planets, and other celestial bodies, over thousands of years, led to the development of the first calendars and ultimately to the ability to predict the positions of the planets and the sun with astonishing accuracy. In the 16th century, this led to the Copernican revolution—understanding that the planets rotate around the sun—and later allowed Johannes Kepler to further deduce that the orbits of the planets are in the shape of an ellipse. Astronomical observations were also critical in overturning

Isaac Newton's view of absolute space and time and replacing it with Albert Einstein's theory of relative space-time.

The principle of induction is simple—observations that are repeatable are likely due to some underlying regularity that is there to be discovered. More generally, we observe some distribution of outcomes and look for some explanation as to why that specific distribution has occurred and not some other.

Ultimately, science looks to explain, control, and predict the world around us[5] based on the evidence compiled through induction. It does so by trying to determine the simplest and most powerful explanation for a body of observations. Nowadays, this is frequently achieved using computer models that describe and capture in mathematical terms the behaviour of the physical or biological system of interest. Our models of the solar system and the weather work in this way, as do our models of the brain.

Increasingly, learning algorithms are used to construct new inference rules and causal models from data in large AI systems. Such approaches have been used to solve previously intractable problems in science, such as deducing the shape of a protein based on its chemical composition. Inductive reasoning and model building are, therefore, as important as deductive reasoning as key building blocks for AI. A more mundane example is the spam filter used by your email provider, which may use inductive processes to identify and label potential spam messages.

SEARCH AND OPTIMISATION

Today, when we think of search, we often think of *search engines* such as *Google*, *Bing*, and *DuckDuckGo*, which most of us use every day to find information on the internet. Modern search engines are themselves complex AIs that use tools such as natural language processing, pattern recognition, and analysis of user behaviour, together with sophisticated ranking algorithms, to try to give useful answers to our queries. However, search, more broadly defined, is one of the most fundamental challenges in AI—many of the problems that AI looks to solve, from selecting chess moves to landing a robot rover on Mars, can be characterised as search problems.

To apply search in AI, you first define a *state space* and then follow a search procedure to explore that space and find states that correspond to good solutions. In the early years of AI, people worked with problems where the state space was easy to define, such as traditional board games.

Adversarial games like chess can be thought of as a search within a graph (see Figure 4.1, left). The starting state is the first node in the graph, and each possible move takes you to a new node connected to

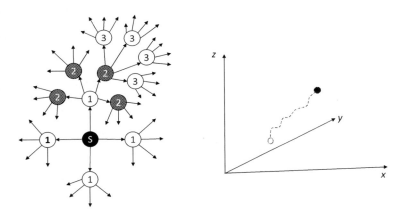

Figure 4.1 Two forms of search. *Left.* Graph search for an adversarial game. From the starting state, S, there are four possible first moves illustrated here (1). I have illustrated the subsequent move (2) by the adversary for just one of these moves, and the third move (3) by the player. Even with just four possible moves, the number of possible states (nodes in the graph) grows very quickly. *Right.* A continuous state-space for an optimisation problem. The dimensions (x, y, and z, here) could correspond to the parts of the solution space for landing a Mars rover. The black dot illustrates the optimal solution, and the white dot is a starting point. The goal of the optimisation process, which is a form of search for continuous state spaces, is to move from the starting point to the optimal solution, ideally along a reasonably direct trajectory such as that illustrated by the dotted line. For most optimisation problems, including landing planetary rovers, there are many more than three dimensions, but the state space cannot easily be visualised beyond three.

the starting node by an *edge*. Each new node sprouts new edges and further nodes, and so on. The graph for a game like chess gets very bushy very quickly—after just the first three moves in chess, there are already nearly nine thousand possible states.

In 1950, Claude Shannon, the inventor of information theory and a co-organiser of the Dartmouth Summer School on AI, attempted to calculate the number of possible states in the game of chess.[6] His estimate of 10^{120} suggests that chess has more possible states than atoms in the observable universe. The beyond astronomic size of state spaces for problems that are as straightforward to describe as chess—thirty-two playing pieces on an eight-by-eight grid—shows us that search strategies for AI need to be very good indeed. Even the fastest chess-playing computer cannot afford to explore all the potential paths to the end of the game when selecting the next move. For instance, a chess-playing super-computer that could examine one trillion chess states per second would take one hundred trillion years to look at just 3.15×10^{32} states, a tiny fraction of Shannon's estimate of total possible states. One hundred trillion years is, according to some estimates, when the last light will go out in our expanding universe. Clearly, exhaustive search, even in a well-defined problem space like chess, is not a viable option.

The rapid proliferation of states in many search problems is often referred to as the "combinatorial explosion". In order to combat this challenge and to perform search efficiently in problems with large state spaces, AIs use algorithms that *evaluate* different states as to whether they are relatively better or worse. One simple strategy that is widely used is the *greedy* algorithm. This approach means looking at the possible immediate alternatives and preferring the one that seems to get you closer to the goal. For instance, in chess, putting your opponent in checkmate is the ultimate goal, but taking your opponent's queen could get you a long way.

The greedy strategy is what AI researchers call a *heuristic*, a rule-of-thumb or shortcut that is often useful but cannot be guaranteed to work. People also use heuristics. In solving search problems, research has shown that we often get stuck at the point where we must take a step that seems to take us further away from the solution, even though this may be a necessary move to solve the overall challenge. Game-playing AIs generally look multiple steps ahead to try to avoid this problem.

Graph searching with heuristics works well when each state is well-defined and separable from every other state and there is a finite number of states—even when, as in chess, the number of states might be too large to be precisely calculable. In other kinds of problems, such as landing a Mars rover, the possible states, such as the position and orientation of the robot, and actions, such as the amount of thrust or steering to be applied, are real numbers. In this setting, where there truly are an infinite number of possible states, search is often referred to as *optimisation*. Here, a good solution corresponds to a point or region inside the multi-dimensional space formed by all the state variables. This is easily imagined for a one-, two-, or three-dimensional state-space (see Figure 4.1, right), but the same principles apply even when you have many more dimensions.

In optimisation problems, the evaluation process is often described as applying a *value function, objective function,* or *fitness function.* All of these mean much the same thing—they describe some way of valuing different states of the system in comparison to some target level of performance. In this case, we can also follow a greedy strategy, which in continuous optimisation problems is called *hill-climbing.* This is based on an analogy that sees search as being like moving on a physical landscape where your aim is to get to the highest peak, as illustrated in Figure 4.2. The evaluation you calculate for your current location is your current height on the landscape, and the hill-climbing strategy is simply to look around locally, see which direction is up, and head that way. You might imagine yourself doing something similar if you go for a walk on a hillside on a very foggy day.

Again, hill-climbing is a heuristic because following the local gradient may lead you to a local peak or *local optimum* rather than the highest point on the landscape. This is one reason that human hill climbers get lost in bad weather. This is also a very well-known problem in AI that can prevent algorithms from finding the best solutions.

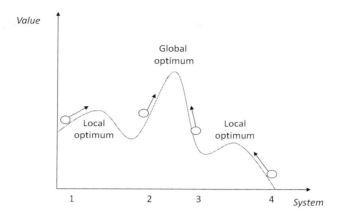

Figure 4.2 Search as hill-climbing. The horizontal axis represents the state space of the system that is being optimised. The solid line shows the *value* function (vertical axis) for every possible position along the horizontal axis. There is one global optimum illustrated here and two local optima. A hill-climbing algorithm would reach the global optimum from starting positions two or three but would end up at a local optimum from positions one or four.

Sometimes, an AI problem is cast as *gradient-descent* rather than hill-climbing. This is the same strategy, but this time, you are saying that the best solutions are the deepest troughs rather than the highest peaks, so you need to move downhill to find better solutions. You can always recast a hill-climbing problem as a gradient-descent one by changing the sign on your evaluation function (turning positive to negative and vice versa), so these really are much the same thing. It is simply more intuitive for some types of problems to talk of maximising something, such as accuracy, reward, or fitness, and for other problems, to talk of minimising something, such as time, energy, cost, or error.

To avoid *local optima* in the solution space—that is, finding a peak but not the highest one—optimisation algorithms use a variety of strategies, such as having multiple starting positions. This means that you can explore multiple possible paths to a goal rather than just one. *Genetic algorithms* inspired by the natural processes underlying evolution use this approach by starting with a population of individuals, each represented by a different artificial chromosome—often just a string of ones and zeroes. Each chromosome is then used to create a candidate solution to the challenge, for example, by using it to build a neural network. That solution is then tested and scored according to its success on the problem at hand. Those solutions that perform best are then copied into the next generation, often using operators such as cross-over (combining sections from two or more chromosomes) and mutation (randomly flipping bits) that are again directly inspired by processes found in biological evolution. Over time, the members of each successive population should get better at the task, eventually achieving scores close to the landscape peaks.

In the 1990s, computer scientist Karl Sims used genetic algorithms to evolve populations of simple articulated creatures controlled by artificial neural networks and moving in simulated physical worlds.[7] Sims showed that he could evolve creatures to be good at locomotion tasks, such as swimming in water or crawling on hard ground. He also found that he could re-create an evolutionary "arms race" by pitting one population of creatures against another on a task such as fighting for control of a resource. Some of Sims' creatures looked and moved in ways that resembled simple animals, illustrating the power of evolution and providing a demonstration of the possibility of "artificial life".

Another strategy for escaping local optima is simply to add noise, or jitter, to your decision rule so that sometimes, just by chance, you take a step that seems to move away from the goal. Adding noise to decision-making seems a rather unintelligent thing to do. However, if you are trying to get better at something, adding some random deviation to what you might otherwise do can be a good way to explore the space of nearby alternative decisions. Evidence from neuroscience suggests that biological neural networks can also be noisy decision-makers. Large language models, such as Open AI's *ChatGPT*, often add a significant element of randomness in their choice of next words as, without noise, their solutions can seem repetitive and banal.

Search and optimisation are such powerful tools that it can be tempting to cast all intelligent behaviour this way. However, these tools have their limits. For instance, in understanding the world, we are often trying to identify features, objects, people, and patterns. It is not always obvious in these domains what measure you are trying to maximise (or minimise). With challenging problems, the hardest task can be to come up with an adequate description of the problem space in which you can then apply search or optimisation.

Sometimes, in AI, researchers study a problem and can devise a direct solution to it through clever mathematics or programming. For example, if you are trying to move a robot, and you know enough about its actuators and joints, then you can write down equations, known as kinematic equations, to say exactly how it should move to reach a particular point in space—no search required. Generally, such approaches can get you a long way and quickly, though you may need to apply optimisation to fine-tune some of the parameters. We typically describe such approaches as engineering rather than as AI; however, there really is no clear distinction. If the human mind is our model for intelligence, then it might have acquired some of these clever direct solutions, too.

PROBABILISTIC REASONING

Consider an example of everyday reasoning. Say you enter a room at a party, just at the moment when someone else is leaving by another door. You catch a glimpse of the departing figure and wonder if it might be your good friend Joe. The figure was tall with long dark hair, as is Joe. They seemed to be wearing a dark leather jacket, which you know is one of Joe's favourite items of attire. Looking around the room, you see Sally, who you know is also a friend of Joe's. Each of these pieces of information is a clue to the possibility that this person you saw might be Joe, but nothing gives you certainty. You might say that the clues add up to make it more than likely that this was Joe, but how does your mind do the adding up exactly?

What your mind is doing is almost certainly some form of probabilistic reasoning, and it is remarkably good at it, even though you might not consider yourself to be gifted in maths. In almost every situation we encounter, we are similarly faced with partial or uncertain information, and our minds must make their best guess as to what is happening. You might be aware of some of this reasoning, but a lot of the time, it is going on in parts of the mind to which you do not have conscious access. We see, with our conscious "mind's eye", the most likely interpretation of the world rather than all the different possibilities that the unconscious mind might be considering. Some optical illusions, such as the duck-rabbit illusion and the Necker cube, both illustrated in Figure 4.3, demonstrate this ambiguity. In inspecting these pictures, the mind flips back and forth between different interpretations, but you can never consciously see both at once. The 19th-century physicist and psychologist Hermann von Helmholtz described what is happening in those parts of the brain to which we do not have conscious access as a form of "unconscious inference".[8]

Probability theory is a branch of mathematics that builds on logic but combines it with number theory. It got going in the 16th century through a famous dialogue between the mathematicians Blaise

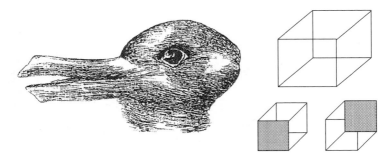

Figure 4.3 Left. A 19th-century drawing of an ambiguous duck-rabbit figure (public domain). Right. The Necker cube illusion. The upper cube is ambiguous and can be seen as consistent with either of the two views shown below. In both drawings, the conscious mind seems to flip between the two possible interpretations, unable to see both at once.

Pascal and Pierre de Fermat about a game of dice. Their efforts formed the foundation of the study of uncertainty. However, the work of a 17th-century vicar, Thomas Bayes, has had arguably the biggest impact on probabilistic reasoning in AI. Bayes, who published no mathematical writings during his lifetime, worked on conditional probabilities—the probability that something will happen on the basis that something else has already happened. His idea led to what is now known as *Bayes rule*,[9] or *Bayesian inference*, a method for chaining together the calculation of probabilities in a similar manner to that considered earlier for chaining sequences of deductions or if-then rules. In this case, though, instead of propagating simple assertions about what is true or false, we are now propagating probabilities, that is, expectations about the likelihood of something being true (or false).

Combining and propagating probabilities requires a lot of calculations, so it was only with the availability of powerful computers that Bayesian approaches really took off. In the 1980s, computer scientist Judea Pearl[10] raised interest in Bayesian reasoning by combining it with graph theory to show how probabilistic inference can be propagated through a network of variables in order to estimate the likelihood of states of interest. In this way, by starting with some known probabilities that you can measure or estimate, you can find out how likely things are that you particularly care about. For instance, in medical diagnosis systems, some nodes might represent test results and symptoms, and other nodes diagnoses. Propagating probabilities through the network could determine which diagnoses were more likely than others—something of real importance to doctors and their patients.

Today, Bayesian inference is one of the core technologies used in many AIs and is a key element of theories of human perception and intelligence that build on Helmholtz's notion of unconscious inference. For example, a recent study by the neuroscientist William Harrison and colleagues[11] found that brain activity related to the encoding of visual orientation was better matched by a Bayesian statistical model than alternative coding schemes. This is evidence that the unconscious mind really might think in terms of probabilities.

More broadly, much of the AI we have today uses methods grounded in statistical (i.e., probabilistic) approaches to finding patterns in data. This is true of many of the approaches that use artificial neural networks, where it can be shown that the behaviour of the network approximates some known statistical method. For instance, some forms of unsupervised learning work because they approximate the statistical method of factor analysis first described by Charles Spearman and discussed in Chapter 2 as a way of identifying different aspects of intelligence from IQ test results. This insight opens the door to understanding the biological neural networks that make up the brain as powerful forms of statistical processing, as we will explore in Chapter 5.

CONTROL THEORY

Remember how before there was AI, there was cybernetics? Before the development of powerful digital computers, a group of researchers known as cyberneticians used the tools of control theory to try to understand the mind and to construct intelligent machines.

One of the key ideas in control theory is negative feedback. Consider the thermostat in your home. This is a simple form of negative feedback controller. Say you set this to a preferred temperature of 21° Celsius. In control theory, this is called a set-point. If the room temperature goes too high, say 23°, the difference between the actual and preferred temperatures is +2°. The thermostat uses negative feedback, so it uses the negative of this number, -2°, to decide what to do, that is, whether to make the room hotter or colder. This number is known as the error. Your thermostat is a very simple kind of controller that only has two choices—to turn the heating on or off. In this case, it wants to make the room cooler by -2° so the heating is turned off. Twenty minutes later, the temperature has dropped and is now 18°; the difference is -2°, but the (negative) feedback is positive this time (two minuses make a plus), so the heating is turned back on.

You might worry that such a simple device might end up continuously turning the heating on and off, which might reduce energy efficiency or increase wear. You would be right. To avoid this kind of oscillation, known as "hunting", your thermostat has a range of temperatures around the set-point, say plus or minus 1°, known as the *hysteresis* range, where it will take no action.

If this works for home heating, it may also help explain how the brain controls some important physiological variables necessary for life and that you also want to keep within a range. These include things like body temperature, blood glucose, hydration, and blood pressure, to name just a few. The activity of keeping critical life variables within range is called *homeostasis* and was an important part of the inspiration for Ross Ashby's cybernetic device, the *Homeostat*.

Many theories of homeostasis build on the concept of a negative feedback controller. These theories generally involve continuous control rather than simple on-off, as in the example of the thermostat. Continuous control can mean the strength of the control signal is proportional to the size of the error or, to provide a smoother form of control, the sum of errors over time, known as *integral* control. Thus, if you are just a little bit cold, you may feel your hair stand on end, which is a useful mechanism to trap heat and experience a slight shiver. But if your core temperature has dropped significantly, you may feel your muscles spasm much more vigorously in an effort to fight the cold. Negative feedback control can be related to the optimisation strategies discussed earlier in that it can be viewed as a form gradient descent towards the target value.

Staying with the problem of keeping warm, the brain, naturally, has many strategies. As well as erecting body hair and shivering, you may begin to burn body fat. These mechanisms are all regulated in the brain below the level of consciousness—you cannot choose not to shiver. However, once you notice you are shivering, you might decide to put on more clothes or move to a warmer part of the house. These are conscious decisions and require a lot more of your brain, including parts of the cortex, to plan and enact. Even so, some theories in psychology still see these behaviours as driven by forms of feedback control. One influential theory, developed in the 1950s by the medical physicist William Powers,[12] proposed that all behaviour is generated by a hierarchy of control loops, with simpler loops driving behaviours such as shivering and more complex ones driving the search for a woolly jumper or a hat.

The human body is an efficient regulator of temperature and, when healthy, maintains a consistent 37°. Is this set-point represented somewhere in the brain? Surprisingly, the answer is probably not. Instead, the different mechanisms for maintaining temperature may operate somewhat independently, using different control, sensory, and motor mechanisms, and perhaps each having its own active temperature range. It might be better to think of that steady body temperature of 37° as a "balance point" that emerges through the interaction of all the brain and body systems for temperature regulation.[13]

The notion of set-point has another problem. Some of the variables that the body needs to control do not have a stable target value; instead, they vary with the activity of the body. For example, blood pressure varies throughout the day and needs to be higher during vigorous activity such as exercise than at rest. Physiological variables such as blood pressure vary in a way that anticipates demand, indicating a form of predictive control. Even body temperature can vary. For instance, when you are fighting an infection, your body temperature will rise because the immune system may operate more effectively if the body is slightly warmer.

We have noted the different historical origins of theories of intelligent systems derived from computer science and control theory. The early AI theorists wanted to distinguish their enterprise from that of cybernetics, so they adopted a new label. Even today, AI researchers and control theorists are likely to sit in different university departments. However, it would be a mistake to overlook the tools provided by control theory for understanding human minds or for creating AI. Indeed, when we are working with complex AI artefacts, such as robots, the mathematical tools of control theory are fundamental to how we go about getting these machines to stay upright, move around, and, more generally, display intelligent behaviour.

DO HUMANS THINK DIFFERENTLY?

There are areas of human reasoning and thinking that have been considered to be beyond AI. I will end this chapter by discussing some of the better-known examples.

Let us start with *analogical* reasoning. This is the ability to solve problems by comparing them to situations that have previously been encountered, perhaps in some completely different sphere of endeavour. Examples of scientific discoveries that are said to have been the result of analogical reasoning include Francis Crick and James Watson's discovery of the structure of the DNA molecule and Albert Einstein's theory of special relativity. In both cases, these scientists made progress by "thinking outside the box" and by looking at other problems in chemistry and physics, and in Crick and Watson's case, building physical models to make progress. Analogical thinking seems to involve noticing patterns and similarities between situations that might otherwise seem unconnected. We will see in a later chapter that abstractions are achievable in AI, and this is central to how they solve problems. Matching abstractions across different fields is still challenging for AI, but there is progress in this direction, for instance, in text-to-image generating AIs, as we will find out in Chapter 6.

In the case of Crick and Watson's physical DNA model, which was made of bits of wire and metal, we can consider this an example of "thinking outside of the head", or what the philosopher Andy Clark has called the "extended mind".[14] This is the ability of people to use their environment to extend their thinking abilities—everyday examples include pen and paper, calendars, maps, calculators, mobile phones, and, of course, computers. Undoubtedly, Crick and Watson also understood a lot about cutting-edge science in the areas of biology, chemistry, and physics, which enabled them to make their discovery, so combining that knowledge with the use of some of these external tools brought about their advance. Albert Einstein was a highly visual thinker who, as a teenager, imagined himself running next to a light beam and picturing the waveform as stationary. Einstein also used imaginary scenarios involving high-speed trains and falling elevators to motivate his ideas about relativity.

Another related area of thinking is what philosophers have called abductive reasoning. *Abduction* is distinguished from deduction and induction as it seems to involve reasoning to the best explanation and "beyond the evidence". In human reasoning, abduction may include heuristics, common sense reasoning, and what we call intuition. One heuristic commonly applied is that of parsimony, the search for the simplest and most elegant solution, also known as Occam's razor. Abduction looks a bit like probabilistic reasoning since both are about making the best guess given limited information. The combination of existing AI technologies and appropriate use of heuristics could allow them to reason abductively, although it will be hard to draw strong conclusions here as psychology and philosophy have failed to provide a clear account of what abduction in human reasoning involves.

More broadly, much has been made of human decision-making being driven by factors other than pure rationality. We encountered this idea in Chapter 2, where we saw different ideas of intelligence, including emotional intelligence and Daniel Kahneman's distinction between "fast" and "slow" thinking. Fast thinking was described as automatic, emotional, and often instinctive and unconscious, and contrasted with the more systematic, conscious, and logical nature of slow thinking.

That a process is automatic and unconscious does not rule it out from being rational. As I have discussed previously, our brain does a lot of problem-solving below the level of awareness, but that can be viewed as a form of inference. But what about emotion and instinct? One way to think about these forms of knowledge is as accumulated wisdom acquired through evolution and learning. If you have acquired a good solution to a problem in the past, then why not save it and use it again? In the broadest sense, this is what evolution is able to do by caching or compiling useful solutions in the form of designs for our bodies and brains. If you enact an evolved solution to a challenge— what psychologists would call an *instinct*—then you may be able to do the right thing, but without being able to explain why.

That you may have a "feeling" about the right thing to do may have to do with the nature of emotions. In one sense, at least, these are evaluations of the kind we have already talked about in discussing search and optimisation. Instinctual or acquired evaluations can enable you to assess a situation very quickly and decide if it is good or bad. The neuropsychologist Antonio Damasio studied brain injuries in emotional areas of the brain that led to poor decision-making. He proposed the "somatic marker hypothesis", that brain regions involved in sensing the body can store associations between situations and outcomes that are then experienced as emotions.[15] There are well-understood methods for learning these kinds of evaluations that have been studied in the AI domain of reinforcement learning and are now employed to train some large-scale learning models.

There is still some mystery about emotions because the human experience of an emotion does not really match with this idea of emotion as an evaluation—after all, this could just be a few brain cells firing. However, in animal (and human) bodies, we need to note the close coupling of brain and body states. An evaluation generated in the brain will lead to further effects, including the release of neuromodulators and appropriate physical behaviour—running away, for example, if you are fearful. The experience of an emotion may then have a lot to do with this mixture of assessing and responding to the external situation and then "feeling" your own body react. The intensity of this response is likely to recruit many more of your brain circuits, heightening the experience and making it memorable.

Besides the kinds of compiled intelligence provided by evolution and learning, human reasoning is also guided by heuristics or rules of thumb. However, as we have seen, heuristics are also widely used by AI. Indeed, even when we have a complete mathematical theory of how to reason through a problem to the perfect answer, it turns out that the computations involved may be too costly to be worthwhile or executable in the time available. Much of AI has, therefore, been about finding useful approximations that get you to a useful solution whilst cutting a few computational corners. One of the founders of AI, Herb Simon, whom we met in Chapter 2, noticed that this is true of humans as well. He suggested that we have "bounded rationality",[16] meaning we have limited cognitive resources, time is usually a constraint, and we will generally be happy with a solution that is good enough rather than truly optimal.

Finally, it is often noted that human reasoning can be biased, meaning we do not adopt the most rational solution to a problem, sometimes in a way that seems to go against our best interests. For example, Daniel Kahneman and his collaborator Amos Tversky described something they called "loss aversion".[17] This is the common human tendency to prefer to avoid the penalty of enduring a loss over the benefit of an equivalent gain. Loss aversion can lead to poor economic decisions. For example, inexperienced investors often hold on to stocks that are losing value when it might be better to sell, or they avoid investments seen as overly risky. However, whilst loss aversion may make the typical human into a poor investor, there are other contexts in which this can be seen as a rational strategy. For example, from an evolutionary perspective, losses can be life-threatening, and if the fundamental goal is survival, being risk-averse can be the better strategy.

So, is there really a form of reasoning or thinking that humans have and that AIs might never have? I'm not sure. When we put together large-scale AIs, perhaps with several of the component systems described here, we will get to forms of thinking that look more like analogical reasoning or abduction. I think we will also see AIs that have the equivalent of fast and slow thinking—being able to make quick and cheap decisions based on pattern recognition and evaluations stored through learning but being able to follow up with slower processes of deduction and reasoning to verify whether the decision was right or not. We will explore this further in the chapters ahead.

NOTES

1   Aristotle. (380BC/2016). *Prior Analytics* I.2 (A. J. Jenkinson, Trans.): Scotts Valley, CA: Createspace.

2   Frege, G. (1967). Concept script, a formal language of pure thought modelled upon that of arithmetic. In J. van Heijenoort (Ed.), *From Frege to Gödel:*

A Source Book in Mathematical Logic, 1879–1931. Cambridge, MA: Harvard University Press.

3 Boole, G. (1853/2009). An Investigation of the Laws of Thought, On Which Are Founded the Mathematical Theories of Logic and Probabilities. Cambridge: Cambridge University Press.

4 McCarthy, J., & Hayes, P. (1969). Some philosophical problems from the standpoint of artificial intelligence. In B. Meltzer & D. Michie (Eds.), Machine Intelligence 4. Edinburgh: Edinburgh University Press.

5 For an introduction to this view of science, see Verschure, P. F. M. J., & Prescott, T. J. (2018). A living machines approach to the sciences of mind and brain. In T. J. Prescott et al. (Ed.), The Handbook of Living Machines: Research in Biomimetic and Biohybrid Systems (pp. 15–25). Oxford: Oxford University Press.

6 Claude, S. (1950). Programming a computer for playing chess. Philosophical Magazine, 41(314).

7 Sims, K. (1994). Evolving virtual creatures. Paper presented to the 21st Annual Conference on Computer Graphics and Interactive Techniques. SIGGRAPH '94, July 24–29, Orlando, Florida.

8 Helmholtz, H. (1878/1971). The facts of perception. In R. Kahl (Ed.), Selected Writings of Hermann von Helmholtz. Middletown, CT: Wesleyan University Press.

9 For an introduction to Bayes rule, see Stone, J. V. (2016). Bayes' Rule with Python: A Tutorial Introduction to Bayesian Analysis. Sheffield, UK: Sebtel Press.

10 Pearl, J. (1995). Probabilistic Reasoning in Intelligent Systems: Networks of Plausible Inference. San Francisco, CA: Morgan Kaufmann.

11 Harrison, W. J., Bays, P. M., & Rideaux, R. (2023). Neural tuning instantiates prior expectations in the human visual system. Nature Communications, 14(1), 5320.

12 Powers, W. T. (1973–2005). Behavior: The Control of Perception (2nd ed.). Chicago, IL: Aldine de Gruyter.

13 See Wilson, S. P., & Prescott, T. J. (2022). Scaffolding layered control architectures through constraint closure: insights into brain evolution and development. Philosophical Transactions of the Royal Society of London. B. Biological Sciences, 377(1844), 20200519.

14 Clark, A. (2010). Supersizing the Mind Embodiment, Action, and Cognitive Extension. Oxford: Oxford University Press.

15 Damasio, A. R. (2000). The Feeling of What Happens: Body, Emotions and the Making of Consciousness. London: Vintage Books.

16 Simon, H. A. (1955). A behavioral model of rational choice. Quarterly Journal of Economics, 69(1), 99–118.

17 Tversky, A., & Kahneman, D. (1992). Advances in prospect theory: cumulative representation of uncertainty. Journal of Risk and Uncertainty, 5(4), 297–323.

5

LEARNING IN NEURAL NETWORKS

Artificial intelligence proceeds in waves, with quieter periods in between that are poetically described as "AI winters". In the late 2000s and early 2010s, a new wave began to gather pace. This was the beginning of the era of large-scale artificial neural network models, popularly known as *deep neural networks* or simply *deep learning*.[1]

These kinds of AIs have attracted a lot of public attention, and for good reason. In multiple domains where humans had, until now, exceeded AI, the machines have been catching up and even bettering their human counterparts. This is particularly true in fields that were not classically seen as involving much intelligence at all—our capacity to understand the world through our senses, also known as *perception*.

Going back to Chapter 2, recall how Aristotle distinguished between perception (*aesthesis*) and intellect (*nuos*). This idea of the primacy of intellect persists in some areas of AI to this day, but as we will explore in this chapter, with neural networks, the path to understanding and recreating human-like intelligence has come through perception, and the broader discovery is that what works for perception may work for intellect too.

DOI: 10.4324/9781003088660-5

FROM PERCEPTION TO PERCEPTRON

In the early days of computing, the available technologies lent themselves more to the study of reasoning processes than to dealing with the real world. The first digital computers began to arrive in universities in the late 1940s, but sensory input devices at that time—microphones and early TV cameras—were still analogue. Their outputs were electrical signals that would need to be converted into digital signals before they could be processed by computers. When computer vision research started in the 1960s, researchers were digitising black-and-white line drawings because working with cameras was just too difficult.

In the 1950s, the science of how the brain processes sensory signals was also just getting going. The neuroscientists David Hubel and Torsten Wiesel recorded in the primary visual cortex of an anaesthetised cat while presenting simple patterns of light on a screen in front of its eyes.[2] They found single cortical neurons that were particularly responsive to bars of light presented at different orientations, suggesting the presence of edge-detection cells in the brain. This was useful evidence that the brain does not capture a direct copy of what we see with the eyes and then present that to the mind on some sort of inner screen. Instead, the brain starts to deconstruct the sensory stimulus from the get-go, picking out the useful elements that can inform about what is happening in the world and what to do next. That neurons can act as *feature detectors* to find edges in the visual scene, and from there, to find and recognise objects and so on, is part of this process.

Around the same time Hubel and Wiesel were making their discoveries, a young engineer called Frank Rosenblatt[3] built the first physical device to instantiate an artificial neural network. Known as the *Perceptron* (a combination of *percept*-ion and *neu-ron*), Rosenblatt's machine connected a layer of electronic binary input devices to a decision-making "neuron" in which each input was connected to the decision-maker by a modifiable real-valued weighted connection (see

Figure 5.1, left). The decision-maker also had a modifiable threshold; its output would be one if the weighted sum of the inputs was greater than this threshold and zero otherwise. In other words, it made a binary yes/no decision.

Rosenblatt used an *error-correcting learning rule*, now known as the *perceptron rule*, to train his device on pattern recognition problems, such as the recognition of handwritten letters and digits. Although later devices included an imaging system, in the early prototypes, patterns were fed directly into the computer using perforated cards. So, for example, if the goal was to recognise the letter X, then the Perceptron would be presented with multiple handwritten versions of an X together with exemplars of other letters.

Rosenblatt's training rule used the difference between the *target output* and the *actual output*. There are two ways in which the Perceptron could misclassify an image. First, if the image was not an X and it responded with a one (yes), then the error signal would be negative ($0-1 = -1$). Second, if the image *was* an X and it responded with a zero (no), then the error signal would be positive ($1-0 = +1$). If the classification was correct, the error would be zero, and there would be no change to the weights. Using this learning rule, the Perceptron

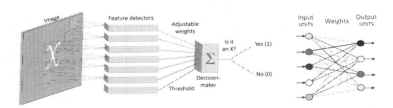

Figure 5.1 *Left*. Rosenblatt's Perceptron. The decision-maker learns to discriminate handwritten letters using weighted inputs from feature-detector units. *Right*. A more generic illustration of a single-layered network. An input pattern is presented on the left and fed through the layer of adjustable connections to generate an output. The connections are modified according to the difference between the target and actual outputs using the delta rule (see text that follows). The activations of the input and output units can be real-valued (typically in the range 0.0–1.0). In single-layer networks, weights are real numbers and can be both positive and negative.

would gradually get better at its task by strengthening weights from feature detectors that consistently fired when an X was present and weakening weights from detectors that fired when X was absent. Over time, there would be fewer and fewer mistakes and fewer non-zero learning signals. Once the Perceptron was correctly classifying all the images, the weights would not change at all. In search terms, you could say that it had completed its gradient descent.

In 1959, two electrical engineers, Bernard Widrow and Ted Hoff,[4] discovered a new learning rule, now known as the *delta rule*, that can be thought of as a generalisation of the perceptron learning rule. The new rule was not restricted to binary inputs and outputs and minimised the sum of the squared errors across all of the patterns in the data set in a way that could be related to methods used by statisticians for finding patterns in data. This meant that, as well as knowing that the learning rule worked, there was a good explanation as to *why* it worked. Widrow and Hoff also developed a hardware classification device called *Adaline* that implemented their learning model. Today, models such as the Perceptron and Adaline are described as belonging to the class of *single-layer neural networks* (see Figure 5.2, right) and are viewed as pioneering steps towards the powerful neural network AIs of the 21st century.

In the late 1950s, there was a great deal of excitement about AI. Rosenblatt's Perceptron, for instance, was hailed by the *New York Times* as "an electronic brain that 'teaches' itself".[5] A second *Times* article, based on a press conference with Rosenblatt himself, talked of an electronic computer that would be "able to walk, talk, see, write, reproduce itself and be conscious of its existence".[6]

Within a decade, though, researchers in AI were turning away from the promise of neural networks and back to less brain-inspired forms of AI. The reason? Single-layer neural networks are unable to resolve many types of classification problems, including some that are relatively easy for people and include a foundational logic circuit known as exclusive-or. This limitation was discussed at length in a famous book entitled *Perceptrons*, published in 1969 by Marvin Minsky and his colleague Seymour Papert.[7] Minsky and Rosenblatt were at high school together but are said to have been rivals, which may help to explain some of Minsky's enthusiasm for deflating Rosenblatt's bubble.

In 1972, a further influential book called *What Computers Can't Do*,[8] authored by the philosopher Hubert Dreyfus, launched a stinging attack on AI, criticising its ability to capture human expert knowledge. Dreyfus argued that human knowledge was contextual, often tacit, and intuitive, and therefore difficult to explain or capture with computer programs. He was dismissive of the possibility that digital computers could be useful for understanding the brain and thought little of Rosenblatt's approach to modelling brain-like neural networks. Dreyfus particularly noted that people are experts at seeing patterns in data, including in our everyday perceptual experience, and that pattern recognition goes beyond physical resemblance and is heavily dependent on context. For Dreyfus, AI was purely passive and disembodied, whereas human intelligence was active, embodied, and engaged. Perception was a holistic activity in which "the meaning of the details" was determined alongside that of the whole.

MACHINE LEARNING AND ANIMAL LEARNING

Prior to, and in parallel with, developments in AI, psychologists were also trying to understand how animals are so successful at learning. For instance, experiments by the behaviourist B. F. Skinner showed that pigeons could be trained to peck at targets for a food reward and could make complex judgements about visual stimuli, including distinguishing between different geometric shapes or abstract patterns.

Skinner was so impressed with these abilities that pigeons were considered as a possible means of controlling guided bombs during World War II. The idea was that a pigeon, trained to recognise a specific military target from photographs, would sit in the nose cone of the bomb and peck at a sensitive screen if the target came into sight, guiding the bomb towards its goal. Pigeon-guided bombs proved impractical and were never deployed in action, but that they were even considered demonstrates the power of visual learning in animals.

In 1972, the psychologists Robert Rescorla and Allan Wagner[9] proposed a learning rule which has been hugely influential in explaining a great many phenomena in animal learning and has since been extended to human perception, category learning, and reasoning. The Rescorla-Wagner rule, as it is now known, was soon recognised as formally equivalent to the Widrow-Hoff delta rule, illustrating the generality of this powerful learning mechanism across both animals and machines. According to Rescorla and Wagner, learning occurs whenever there is a discrepancy between the predicted and actual outcomes (as was also the case in Rosenblatt's learning rule). If an event is *surprising* in the sense that it was not fully expected, learning takes place. If the event is fully predicted, no learning is required.

THE NEW CONNECTIONISM

The scepticism generated by Dreyfus and others, together with the limitations of existing AI systems, led in the 1970s to what is now spoken of as the first AI winter. To be fair, AI had also fallen victim to its own hype as the predictions made by Minsky, Simons, Rosenblatt, and others failed to materialise. But this situation was not to last. In the 1980s, interest in knowledge-based AI was rekindled with the emergence of the first commercial expert systems. During this period, artworks created by AARON, an AI developed by the artist-turned-programmer Harold Cohen, were also widely exhibited, stirring curiosity about the possibility of artificial creativity.[10]

Interest in artificial neural networks also began to re-emerge, partly fostered by the growing interaction between psychologists and AI researchers within the new interdisciplinary field of cognitive science. One of the most exciting findings was the discovery of a way to overcome the limitations of single-layer neural networks by training a multilayer network.

Rosenblatt and the early connectionists knew that a multilayer network could be programmed to solve problems that were insoluble in a single-layer net. The problem had always been how to do that automatically through learning, that is, how to adjust the connections of the network once you had moved beyond the first layer of adaptable weights. In the mid-1980s, David Rumelhart and Robert Williams at the newly founded Department for Cognitive Science in San Diego, California, partnered with the psychologist Geoffrey Hinton to show that it was possible to train a multilayer neural network with an error-correcting learning rule that was a generalisation of the delta rule.[11] The new learning method was called *backpropagation*.

Specifically, starting from the output side of the network, Rumelhart and colleagues showed that you could adjust the output layer of weights as you would do for a single-layer network, then, working backwards through the network, modify the error signal according to the values of the connection weights leading back to each unit in the layer below. For this to work, each artificial neuron (or at least those in the intermediate layers) needed to compute some non-linear function of its input. That is, the output of the unit could not simply be the weighted sum of its inputs (a linear function); instead, it had to be warped in some way (see Figure 5.2, left). This also meant that the intermediate layers of the network—those that were neither input nor output—learned interesting ways of re-representing the inputs that were relevant to solving the problem at hand. In other words, this was a way to design feature detectors automatically without having to code them by hand.

Backpropagation of error quickly became known as *backprop*. Using backprop, researchers showed that the simple problems that Minsky and Papert had pointed to as impossible for a one-layer network could now be solved. Perhaps as importantly, the new "connectionists" took advantage of the increasing power and speed of computers to show that multilayer networks could learn interesting tasks that, up till that point, only people had been good at.

For example, reading aloud was challenging for AI programs because pronunciation, for a language such as English, is not phonetic. There are no simple rules that map spelling to sound, and even when you find a rule, there are often exceptions. For example, in English, "gave", "rave", and "save" all have a similar pronunciation but "have" is different (and for no obvious reason). This meant that reading aloud was difficult to capture using a rule-based approach.

Terry Sejnowksi and Charles Rosenberg's NETtalk model,[12] published in 1987 and shown in Figure 5.2 (right), learned to read and pronounce almost to the level of proficiency of an adult speaker. When fully trained, NETtalk achieved 95% pronunciation accuracy on a test set of several hundred words. Not bad for a model with around three hundred artificial neurons that had learned to read from scratch in just a few days. Interestingly, as it learned, NETtalk made errors similar to those made by beginner human readers, raising the possibility that multilayer networks were doing something brain-like.

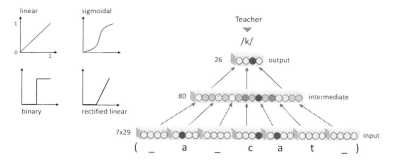

Figure 5.2 *Left.* Four different activation functions that are used in artificial neural networks. Each graph shows the relationship between the input to the artificial neuron (horizontal axis), usually the weighted sum of its inputs from other neurons, and the output of the neuron (vertical axis). The perceptron used a binary decision rule; multilayer networks require smoothly varying, non-linear activation functions such as the sigmoid or the rectified linear function (popular in recent deep learning models). *Right.* NETtalk was a multilayer network developed by Sejnowksi and Rosenberg to read text aloud. Each artificial neuron has an adjustable connection to every unit in the layer above (summarised by arrows). The input layer inspects a seven-letter window of text. There are twenty-nine cells for each letter position corresponding to twenty-six letters of the alphabet, space, and some punctuation marks. The network is tasked with pronouncing the sound at the centre of the window, in this case, the /k/ of "cat". The units in the output layers correspond to twenty-six possible sounds (phonemes); the correct phoneme should be activated, and all others should be inactivated. The teaching signal indicates the correct phoneme. All connections were adjusted by backpropagation. The cells in the intermediate layer learned to form a representation of the written input suitable for selecting the correct phoneme.

THE THIRD WAVE

As noted at the start of this chapter, a further wave of excitement about AI began in the late 2000s, again triggered by progress in neural networks. What had happened in the two decades since the discovery of backprop was, of course, the development of more and more powerful computers. With the advent of the internet, there was also a massive amount of easily accessible, human-generated content that could be harvested to train neural networks. Hardware accelerators such as graphics processors and the computer server farms that technology companies such as Google and Facebook were building to support the rise of the internet also allowed researchers to build and train larger and larger models with more and more data.

Perception was again a key target, but now the problem of translating from analogue to digital was gone. All content, particularly video and audio, was in the digital domain, some of it in easy-to-manipulate databases. This was also the beginning of the age of "big data", and companies were learning about the usefulness of having data that was well structured and labelled, usually by humans, to say what that content was. In areas such as speech recognition and computer vision, the challenges were being redefined based on these large datasets. The outputs of human coding provided the gold standard, and the task was to see how close you could get.

Another idea that was borrowed from biology was the notion of a *convolutional neural network* (CNN). As mentioned in Chapter 2, vision is processed in multiple areas of the brain, but with a common feature that the spatial organisation of the visual world is largely preserved. That is, nearby parts of space are processed by neighbouring regions of the retina and the same all the way up through the visual processing layers of the cerebral cortex. This type of organisation, termed *topographic*, suggests that, at each level, neighbouring groups of cells may perform similar computations on the inputs arriving from local areas in the layer below. In an artificial convolutional network, this idea is implemented by having a single set of adjustable weights that is applied across all local regions of the network at each layer.

The network moves across the image, region by region, in a process known as *convolution*. Doing the same computation across all local areas of the image saves on the number of adaptive weights needed. This also means you can learn faster as all regions of the image can contribute to training a single set of weights.

Since the 1980s, there have been significant improvements and tweaks to learning algorithms such as backpropagation enhancing their efficiency. There is now a better understanding of how these algorithms work. The broader field of machine learning also encompasses probabilistic methods such as Bayesian inference. However, there has been continuing debate as to whether AI has the right learning algorithms. Whilst backpropagation is effective, the question arises could another learning algorithm be more accurate, better at generalising, or faster at learning? As it turns out, one key breakthrough was simply to build bigger and deeper neural networks, that is, ones with both more artificial neurons and more layers; two developments that make artificial neural networks more brain-like.

The cumulative effects of these improvements and the capacity to train bigger and deeper models gradually emerged in the 2000s, but the new deep learning methods really hit the headlines towards the end of that decade. One leap forward around 2009 was that speech models using neural networks moved ahead of those working on other principles.[13] Another area was computer vision. In 2012, *Alex-Net*,[14] a deep learning neural network developed by Alex Krizhevsky, Ilya Sutskever, and Geoffrey Hinton (one of the earlier discoverers of backprop), won a major annual pattern recognition competition in computer vision. This contest required algorithms to correctly classify thousands of different objects, such as animals, buildings, food, man-made artefacts, and natural elements, such as trees and clouds, and so on. The training set was pre-labelled and consisted of millions of images. AlexNet, whose architecture is shown in Figure 5.3, is an eight-layer convolutional neural network with 650,000 artificial neurons and sixty million parameters. When tested in the 2012 competition, it made fewer than half as many mistakes as its closest rival.

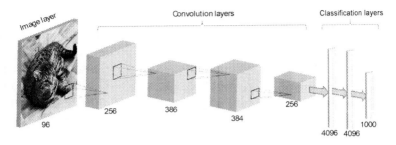

Figure 5.3 AlexNet is an example of a deep convolutional neural network for classification and pattern recognition. The eight-layer network includes four convolution layers and a three-layer classification network that classifies the image into one of a thousand different categories. Numbers indicate how many artificial neurons are in each layer.

ARE DEEP NEURAL NETWORKS REALLY BRAIN-LIKE?

Convolutional neural networks like AlexNet are inspired by the brain, but is processing in the brain anything like that in a deep neural network? There are reasons to think that it might be.

One is that when we look at what is learned in a deep network trained for visual pattern recognition, we see that individual artificial neurons are acquiring some of the feature-detector properties that we see in biological neurons.[15] In the lower layers of such a network, that is, those nearest to the camera image, artificial neurons typically develop response characteristics that correspond to simple features such as detecting blobs (light patches with a darker surround), edges, or simple geometric patterns such as grids and corners. Similar responses have been found in the retinal ganglion cells at the back of the eye and in the primary visual cortex, as seen, for instance, in Hubel and Wiesel's experiments. Artificial neurons in the higher levels of a deep network, in other words, those closer to making a classification decision, have feature detector properties that are much more complex. For example, these might respond to complex shapes, textures, or irregular patterns, to parts of an object, or even to whole objects. Similarly, as you move upstream in visual pathways of the brain, researchers have also found neurons with more and more complex response properties.

Another characteristic that some deep network models share with the brain is a pyramid-like organisation. Here, the largest arrays of artificial neurons are those closest to the image, whilst those closest to the classification layer often have fewer neurons. This means there may be a poorer resolution at the higher layers, but this can also improve the ability of the network to generalise, for instance, recognising objects anywhere in the image (a property known as spatial invariance). As we move upstream in the visual pathways of the brain, there is a similar down-scaling. For example, we noted earlier that there is one retinal ganglion cell for every ten rod or cone cells; for every seven retinal ganglion neurons, there is also just one neuron in the V1 area of primary visual cortex.

A further question is whether the brain uses anything like the back-propagation learning algorithm. When researchers initially looked at this, they were sceptical. The brain seemed to be lacking the right kind of backward-projecting connections to allow the propagation of errors. More recently, evidence has come to light suggesting that something that approximates backpropagation of error could be happening in the brain.[16] Furthermore, success in training large models has also been achieved with unsupervised and reinforcement learning, some of which are strongly inspired by learning mechanisms found in biological neural circuits. With these methods, there is also no need for human labelling of the training data.

Of course, artificial neural networks are different in a great many ways from the neural circuits of the brain, and some researchers will argue that the differences may be more important than the similarities. I am less sure—at a functional level, these deep neural network models seem to be getting a lot of things right.

AlexNet and similar breakthroughs presaged a widespread move to using deep network technologies in AI, particularly in challenges of machine perception that involve pattern recognition, achieving beyond human levels of performance in tasks such as face recognition, image classification, and medical imaging.

The success of deep networks suggests that the early promise of learning in brain-like AI models is being fulfilled, despite the longer-than-expected wait and early scepticism. Strikingly, these networks appear to operate in the kind of holistic way that Dreyfus was looking for—resolving the wider question "What is it?" at the same time as deciding the details. But are there areas of AI where neural network technologies might not succeed? One candidate could be language, one of the capabilities that most distinguishes humans from other animals. We will explore this next.

LARGE-LANGUAGE MODELS: A BREAKTHROUGH IN AI?

Ever since its beginning, one of the key challenges for AI has been to understand and use human language. As noted in Chapter 2, this was also Alan Turing's challenge to AI—could a machine have a conversation with a human without that person knowing that they were talking to an artefact? That no other animal has developed a form of communication as sophisticated as human language also makes this a special problem and one that appeals to our most deep-rooted intuitions about the unique nature of human intelligence. Remember the WAIS intelligence test and its four sub-scales (described in Chapter 2)? These were verbal comprehension, working memory, perceptual organisation, and processing speed. As we have seen, AI is already challenging humans on memory, perception, and processing power. If AI could crack the language challenge, then the notion that machines could never match human intelligence would lose one of its central pillars.

There is some evidence that the breakthrough has already come. In 2023, I can have a meaningful (to me) conversation with an artificial neural network model of language. Indeed, as I write, I am having a side conversation with ChatGPT 3.5, where I am getting its help in following some of the history of AI and in thinking about some of the key ideas in AI and how they relate to each other. Of course, I am aware that ChatGPT can make mistakes; I have spotted a few and carefully checked with other sources. However, it is largely on the money. As a way of getting useful information fast, it certainly adds to my repertoire of "extended mind" tools alongside search engines, databases, e-papers, e-books, and the occasional printed volume from my bookcase.

The ability to use language shown by ChatGPT and other large language models has surprised many people, including me. There are reasons to be impressed. In 2023, a clinical psychologist, Eka Roivainen, an assessment psychologist who routinely tests human intelligence, gave ChatGPT the WAIS test for verbal IQ.[17] There was no special treatment—Roivainen cut and pasted the questions from the test and marked the answers as you would for a human participant. ChatGPT "aced" the test, according to Roivainen. Averaged across the five verbal IQ tests in the WAIS scale, ChatGPT had a verbal IQ of 155—better than 99.9% of the 2,450 people who had been tested when the scale was standardised. How did neural networks become so good at language (at least according to this standard psychological benchmark)? We need to look back at the history of research on natural language processing in AI to find out.

DOES LANGUAGE REQUIRE RULES?

Early progress in AI suggested that the problem of processing natural language would require a rule-based solution. The linguist and cognitive scientist Noam Chomsky had famously critiqued behaviourist theories of language, such as those of B. F. Skinner, for failing to explain linguistic productivity, that is, the ability of language speakers to generate sentences that have never been said before. According to Chomsky,[18] the mind must have some complex, innate, and language-specific processing systems to acquire and use language; that is, you are born already knowing the set of grammatical rules, termed *universal grammar*, that underlies all human languages.

Researchers investigating rule-based AI were also quick to write off the neural networks of Rosenblatt's era as too simple to be interesting.

These models were solely about learning "associations", an idea that had originated with Aristotle (as we saw in Chapter 2). Associative learning was also at the heart of the behaviourists' theories, including, of course, the Rescorla-Wagner learning rule. Clearly, while learning had its place in explaining how pigeons learn to peck at shapes on screens, it seemed that smart learning rules could never be enough to solve language. How could a system that learns by rote ever come up with an original sentence?

Language also seemed to be obviously constrained by grammatical rules. For instance, take the sentence, "The boy who was chasing the dog tripped over the cat". What is the verb "tripped" referring to here? Is it the dog, or the boy, or even the cat? Of course, it is the boy (and also the cat), as many four-year-olds could tell you. According to linguists such as Chomsky, you know this because your brain deconstructs this sentence to discover that it includes the embedded clause "who was chasing the dog". Your knowledge of the structure of language allows you to put that embedded clause to one side while processing the rest, leaving you to understand the simpler construction "the boy . . . tripped over the cat". Your brain also knows about different classes of words. For instance, it knows that verbs like "trip" need a subject which is a noun, in this case, "the boy", and an object which is also a noun, in this case, "the cat". Finally, your brain also knows that if the chasing happened in the past ("was") then the tripping must have also happened then, too, hence the second use of the past tense ("tripped").

All of this speaks to the systematic nature of language and to the need for the mind to know language rules, but where, in a neural network, could the rules of universal grammar reside? For Jerry Fodor, a colleague of Chomsky's at MIT's Department of Brain and Cognitive Sciences, the problem was that neural networks were *subsymbolic*; they could not capture the idea of *symbols* as standing in for concepts.[19] For Fodor, the systematicity and productivity we find in human language were also critical for other areas of thinking and reasoning. The mind, he supposed, must use its own private symbolic code to represent and manipulate concepts and to perform thinking; he termed this internal symbol system the "language of thought".[20]

At first sight, the arguments from the language theorists seemed convincing. Even in a complex network like NetTalk that can learn to read, there is just a forest of weighted connections and nothing that looks like rules. That NetTalk only scored 95% on its test set left an open question: could the difference be due to the human mind's knowledge of pronunciation rules?

The debate between the "symbolists" (like Fodor) and the connectionists was further stirred from the connectionist side. The connectionists argued that the brain uses soft constraints as encoded by network weights, rather than hard-and-fast rules. Moreover, this was not just "associationism". The capacity of hidden neurons to create new kinds of internal representations made connectionist models "cognitive" and more powerful than the earlier learning theories of behaviourists. There was a kind of internal code in the brain, but it took the form of massively distributed and continuously changing patterns of activation. In 1989, David Rumelhart, one of the inventors of backprop, wrote, "our goal, in short, is to replace the computer metaphor with the brain metaphor".[21] This was a turf war. The aim of the connectionists was to explain everything about the mind, and language was the key battleground.

LEARNING LANGUAGE WITH RECURRENT NETWORKS

In the 1980s and early 1990s, when the debate between symbolic and subsymbolic AI was at its fiercest, the jury was still out as to who had the better account of how the brain solves language. However, important work was going on that showed the promise of neural network technologies, even though there was a long way to go before we would have useful network-driven language processing tools. One important set of clues came from research on recurrent neural networks.

A recurrent network is one in which the output of the network (at some level) can flow back and influence its own future input. This contrasts with the feed-forward networks most often explored in AI, including many of the deep neural network models used today, in which signals flow in only one direction through the network, from input to output, and never the other way (except for adjusting the connections).

There are many reasons to be interested in recurrent networks. One is that in biological neural systems, there is a great deal of recurrence—our brains are full of local networks sending signals to other networks and receiving signals back, often all at the same time. Even in the perceptual pathways of the brain discussed earlier, information is flowing in both directions, something that is not captured in most current deep network models. For instance, in the visual system, higher cortical areas project back towards lower ones, including the primary visual cortex.

Another reason to explore recurrent networks is that they are useful for understanding processing that happens over time. Activity in the brain inevitably has a temporal dimension because its primary challenge is to cope, in real-time, with the ever-changing world. In the brain circuits that generate behaviour, recurrence is also a common finding, particularly for cyclic behaviours such as walking, swimming, or breathing. Indeed, anywhere in the brain that generates patterned activity is likely to be exploiting recurrence.

An important example of a process that generates patterned activity over time is, of course, language. When you are listening or speaking, you hear or generate words in sequence. Even when you are reading, you will go in sequence from the beginning of the paragraph to its end, even though it might be possible, when reading quickly, to interpret a chunk of text bigger than one word in one go.

In language, as in many other sequential processes, what has come before is important for understanding what is happening now. So, for a neural network to understand language, it must be able to keep track of content that was encountered earlier in the interaction; in other words, it must have memory. Recurrent neural networks can provide a form of memory by feeding information from the output side of the network back into the inputs. This process can "keep alive" relevant information from the earlier part of the interaction without having to store everything that has been said.

Researchers in rule-based AI were also well aware of the power of recurrence. Indeed, rule-based models in AI, including formal models of natural language, make extensive use of rules that are recursive, that is, that call themselves. Entire AI programming languages, such as Lisp and Prolog, were specifically designed to make easy use of the power of recursion.

In the second wave of connectionism, in the 1980s, people were already starting to investigate the potential of recurrent neural networks. An important question was to see if it was practically possible to use recurrent networks to generate sequential behaviour, and to act as short-term memories. If so, could they be applied to the ultimate challenge of learning language?

In the early 1990s, Jeffry Elman joined the Cognitive Science department in San Diego to attempt this challenge. One of the problems he chose to study was a highly simplified version of the English language. Specifically, Elman decided to train a simple recurrent network with just over two hundred artificial neurons and just under three thousand adjustable connections on a large number of sentences of between three and sixteen words, but all constructed using a very limited vocabulary of just twenty-three words.[22]

The task for Elman's network was to predict the next word in the sentence, and it was trained to get better at this using backprop. In other words, every time the network predicted the wrong word, there would be error feedback, and the learning algorithm would make small changes to all the connection strengths in the network. Elman's hypothesis was that if the network was able to learn this task, this would mean that it had internalised something important about the structure of language.

Elman's network was able to learn the prediction task he had set, as illustrated in Figure 5.4. Note that the network has intermediate layers that form distributed representations of the words in the sentence, with a set of "context" units that recycle the output of one of the intermediate layers to be part of its own input on the next time-step. The input and output layers use exactly the same representation, with one unit standing for each of the twenty-three words (and a

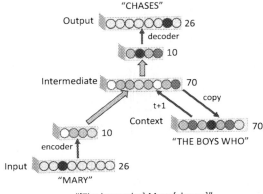

Figure 5.4 Elman's simple recurrent network. Numbers indicate how many artificial neurons are in each layer. Only the connections indicated by the block arrows are adjustable. The network is processing the sentence "The boys who Mary chases" and has reached the word "Mary". The phrase "The boys who" is represented in the context units that are recurrently linked into the intermediate layer. The output layer correctly predicts that the next word (out of a possible twenty-three) should be "chases".

few extra units for non-words) and with a fixed encoding/decoding layer at each end that converts this into/from a distributed activation pattern.

After training, Elman presented each possible input word to the network and recorded the activation pattern that was formed in the intermediate layer. By comparing these patterns for different words, he was able to show that his network learned to cluster certain types of words that play similar roles in sentences. For instance, nouns shared similarities to each other in the way they were represented in the network, while verbs also formed their own cluster. More than that, different types of nouns tended to cluster together. For instance, nouns like human names or animal names formed a cluster, as these often provide the actor, or "subject", in a sentence. At the same time, nouns that related to inanimate objects also clustered—these nouns relate to items that are often acted upon, serving as the "object" in a sentence.

Elman also found that his network was able to encode some long-distance grammatical dependencies. For instance, in the sentence "the girl who chased the dog that bit the boy likes ice-cream", the network was able to correctly predict a singular verb, "likes", to go with a singular subject, "the girl", that had appeared nine words earlier. This is specifically something that the symbolic theorists had said connectionist models would struggle to do.

Notice that Elman's network was only trained to predict the next word; it was given no training at all about grammatical types like nouns and verbs or subjects and objects. Simply by learning to predict, the network implicitly acquired knowledge that can be related to these grammatical concepts. Notice also that the network did not literally learn the rules of grammar; instead, it learned hundreds of connection weights whose behaviour can be described approximately using formal grammar. For another connectionist, Paul Smolensky,[23] this subsymbolic level of representation stands in relation to the rule-based theories of Chomsky and others, like the relationship between quantum mechanics and the classical Newtonian laws of motion in physics. Newtonian physics provides a useful but inexact account of how motion happens in the world, but quantum mechanics gives a deeper and more accurate picture. For Smolensky, rule-based theories might work as an approximation to what was happening in the brain, but if you want to fully understand how intelligence emerges from the brain, you need to go down a level.

LARGE LANGUAGE MODELS

Elman's recurrent network, with just three thousand adjustable weights, showed that it was possible, in principle, to discover the structure of grammar simply by learning to predict the next word in the sentence. Remarkably, *large language models* (LLMs), such as Open AI's ChatGPT, Google's PaLM, and Meta's LLama, use much the same trick, but this time with all the power and scale of modern deep learning. For example, ChatGPT 3.5 has 175 billion parameters, around sixty million times larger than Elman's network and around three thousand times bigger than AlexNet.

LLMs belong to the wider class of *generative* AI models that learn to generate new data that could belong to the dataset on which they were trained. In the case of LLMs, these models are trained on huge databases of human-generated text harvested from the internet. As we have already noted, the ability of LLMs to generate new text means that AI can now claim to have achieved human-level performance on tests of verbal intelligence. We will use the current free version of OpenAI's LLM, ChatGPT 3.5, to explore how these powerful AIs work.

In the early 2010s, researchers were experimenting with ever-larger recurrent networks for language processing using Elman's unsupervised method of training where the goal of the network is to predict the next word. The primary value of recurrence in language is the ability to retain a trace of relevant earlier parts of the text—a form of working memory and selective attention. In 2015, Ashish Vaswani and a team of researchers at Google[24] discovered that similar results could be achieved by keeping past elements of the sequence as inputs to the network and, instead of recurrence, using a fully feed-forward attentional mechanism known as a *transformer*. The transformer acts like the playback head on a tape machine, selecting one part of the tape—here, the sequence of words—to attend to at any time. A multi-headed transformer model allows sustained attention to many earlier parts of the sequence, with attention switching, as needed, as the text is processed. Transformer models are central to how ChatGPT works; indeed, the GPT part of the name ChatGPT stands for "Generative Pre-trained Transformer".

When ChatGPT processes text, it takes the sequence of words and converts that into an activation pattern across many thousands of artificial neurons encoding what words are present and their positions within the sequence. Strictly speaking, the model works with parts of words, called *tokens*, by deconstructing words into sub-words that might be informative and help the network to generalise. For instance, "colourful" might be tokenised as "colour" and "ful", or "wandered" as "wander" and "ed". With ChatGPT 3.5, the input pattern can encode up to 4,096 sequential tokens (version 4 remembers up to 32,000 tokens). This input is passed through ninety-six transformer layers, each composed of a mixture of attention heads and feed-forward networks. The model then generates an output, which is a prediction of possible next tokens. This is compared to the actual next token in the text stream, and like Elman's network, the difference is used to train the transformer layers using backpropagation of errors. In other words, as in many neural networks, the generalised delta rule is used to perform gradient descent in the parameter space of the network.

Note that ChatGPT, like other contemporary LLMs, does not simply predict the next token. Instead, it attaches a probability to all possible tokens. When used for language generation, this leaves some other mechanism to decide which token to use for the current task. When Alec Radford and colleagues[25] at OpenAI began to develop the ChatGPT series of language models, they found that this kind of network, once it is trained, can be usefully combined with supervised or reinforcement learning systems for fine-tuning or to address specific language tasks. For instance, OpenAI trained extensions to their model that could summarise text, perform common-sense reasoning, and classify sentences (for instance, as grammatical or non-grammatical).

One such extended version of ChatGPT is OpenAI's online chatbot, which takes a series of prompts from the user and generates a textual response each time. Here, an additional mechanism selects a specific token from the probability distributions of possible tokens generated by the core model. The selected token then becomes part of the input to the model that is used to generate subsequent tokens. Note that by including its own output in the revised input sequence, the model is implementing a form of recurrence.

Using ChatGPT allows the chatbot to create sentences and paragraphs that have never been written before. In order not to be too predictable, the text-generating part of the chatbot may inject a moderate amount of noise into the process of selecting tokens. This is a parameter that can be varied, but experiments have shown that a probability of around 0.8 for selecting the most likely token (in other words, a one in five chance of selecting a less likely token) gives a good balance between being on topic without too much repetition of words or ideas.

Let us look at some output from ChatGPT 3.5. I entered the following instruction into a new session: "Write a sonnet in the style of William Shakespeare about the love between a fiddle player and his robot dog". This is what I got back:

Upon the stage where shadows gently dance,
A fiddler's fingers weave a tender spell,
His melody, a whispered sweet romance,
With strings that hum, a tale of love to tell.

Beside him stands a creature forged of steel,
A faithful hound, with circuits and with gears,
Yet in its eyes, a warmth that seems so real,
A loyal heart, unmarred by mortal fears.

Together they create a sonnet rare,
The fiddle's sighs, the robot's quiet hum,
A duet played with passion and with care,
As if two souls in perfect unison.

In silicon and strings, love finds its way,
A fiddler and his robot dog at play.

The rules of sonnet writing, which are quite strict, are followed accurately here, including the rhyme scheme ABAB CDCD EFEF GG. Whether you like this poem or not is a matter of taste. Some readers, I am sure, will consider it bathos. I found it quite touching, if a little clichéd. But whether you consider it poetry or (robot) doggerel, I hope you can still recognise the achievement. This is almost certainly the first poem ever composed about love between a fiddle player and a robot dog, so there is some originality here—maybe even creativity.

ChatGPT knows no explicit language rules and has learned about poetry, rhyme, love, fiddlers, and robots only from existing examples of human language output. Attending to others, though, is also, in large part, how humans learn their own native tongue. Chomsky and Fodor argued that considerable language-specific innate knowledge was needed to acquire language, including some universal grammar. Here we have a system with almost no prior language knowledge, and certainly no grammar, that has learned to create original passages of text that are organised, grammatical, and meaningful (to us humans).

But are generative AIs, like ChatGPT, simply very large programs that mimic aspects of human intelligence but still lack the key ingredients to match or surpass it? We will consider this question and what, if anything, could be missing in the next chapter.

NOTES

1 LeCun, Y., Bengio, Y., & Hinton, G. (2015). Deep learning. *Nature*, 521(7553), 436–444.

2 Hubel, D. H., & Wiesel, T. N. (1962). Receptive fields, binocular interaction and functional architecture in the cat's visual cortex. *Journal of Physiology*, 160, 106–154.

3 Rosenblatt, F. (1958). The perceptron: a probabilistic model for information storage and organization in the brain. *Psychological Review*, 65(6), 386–408.

4 Widrow, B., & Hoff, M. E. (1960). Adaptive switching circuits. In *IRE WESCON Convention Record* (Vol. Part 4, pp. 96–104). New York: IRE.

5 Quote from www.nytimes.com/1958/07/13/archives/electronic-brain-teaches-itself.html

6 Quote from www.nytimes.com/1958/07/08/archives/new-navy-device-learns-by-doing-psychologist-shows-embryo-of.html

7 Minsky, M., & Papert, S. (1972/1988). *Perceptrons* (3rd ed.). Cambridge, MA: MIT Press.

8 Dreyfus, H. L. (1972). *What Computers Can't Do: A Critique of Artificial Reason*. New York: Harpers and Row.

9 Rescorla, R. A., & Wagner, R. A. (1972). A theory of Pavlovian conditioning. In *Classical Conditioning II: Current Theory and Research* (pp. 64–99). New York: Appleton-Century-Crofts.

10 For details, see https://computerhistory.org/blog/harold-cohen-and-aaron-a-40-year-collaboration/

11 Rumelhart, D. E., Hinton, G. E., & Williams, R. J. (1986). Learning representations by back-propagating errors. *Nature*, 323(6088), 533–536.

12 Sejnowski, T. J., & Rosenberg, C. R. (1987). Parallel networks that learn to pronounce English text. *Complex Systems*, 1, 145–168.

13 Reviewed in Hinton, G. et al. (2012). Deep neural networks for acoustic modeling in speech recognition: the shared views of four research groups. *IEEE Signal Processing Magazine*, 29(6), 82–97.

14 Krizhevsky, A., Sutskever, I., & Hinton, G. E. (2017). ImageNet classification with deep convolutional neural networks. *Commun. ACM*, 60(6), 84–90.

15 See Güçlü, U., & van Gerven, M. A. J (2015). Deep neural networks reveal a gradient in the complexity of neural representations across the ventral stream. *Journal of Neuroscience*, 35(27), 10005–10014.

16 Lillicrap, T. P. et al. (2020). Backpropagation and the brain. *Nature Reviews Neuroscience*, 21(6), 335–346.

17 Roivainen, E. (2023). AI's IQ. *Scientific American*, 329, 7.

18 Chomsky, N. (1968). *Language and the Mind*. Cambridge: Cambridge University Press.

19 Fodor, J. A., & Pylyshyn, Z. W. (1988). Connectionism and cognitive architecture: a critical analysis. *Cognition*, 28, 3–71.

20 Fodor, J. (1976). *The Language of Thought*. Hassocks, Sussex: Harvester Press.

21 Rumelhart, D. E. (1989). The architecture of mind: a connectionist approach. In *Foundations of Cognitive Science*. (pp. 133–159). Cambridge, MA: MIT Press.

22 Elman, J. L. (1990). Finding structure in time. *Cognitive Science*, 14(2), 179–211.

23 Smolensky, P. (1988). On the proper treatment of connectionism. *Behavioural and Brain Sciences*, 11, 1–74.

24 Vaswani, A. et al. (2017). Attention is all you need. *arXiv:1706.03762*.

25 Radford, A., Narasimham, K., Salimans, T., & Sutskever, I. (2018). Improving language understanding by generative pre-training. *OpenAI Blog*.

6

TOWARDS ARTIFICIAL GENERAL INTELLIGENCE

The performance of deep learning and generative AIs is impressive and represents major breakthroughs in some of the most difficult problems for AI. However, some people are unconvinced that this is real intelligence. We will explore this question further in this chapter and discuss what else AI might need to do if it is to match or exceed human intelligence. We will also consider what some AI researchers have described as building *Artificial General Intelligence*, or AGI, a form of AI that is intended to be as flexible as human intelligence in its ability to work across different domains and to adapt to new challenges.

ARE LARGE-SCALE AIS LEARNING ANYTHING INTERESTING?

First, let us consider one critique of current AI, in the form of generative AI, and particularly large language models (LLMs). The suggestion is that these models are not as smart as they appear and are exploiting brute force computing power and huge memory capacity to give an appearance of intelligence. This critique has been made by the writer, psychologist, and sometimes AI sceptic Gary Marcus, who wrote in 2022: "In GPT-3's case the *mechanism* of the prediction is essentially regurgitation; such systems are trained on literally

DOI: 10.4324/9781003088660-6

billions of words of digital text; their gift is in finding patterns that match what they have been trained on".[1] This kind of pattern-matching resembles what Dreyfus critiqued in the 1970s as matching for "physical resemblance" which he considered to be inadequate to explain human intelligence (see Chapter 4).

You might imagine, based on the huge size of these models, that this kind of glorified "table lookup" could be possible. For instance, ChatGPT 3.5 has 175 billion parameters. Could this simply be storing lots of useful chunks of text that are then spliced together to make plausible answers? This is, after all, how early chatbots worked by pattern matching on target words in the prompt, then using that specific pattern to search for suitable answers in a large table. One of the first chatbots, "Eliza", created by Joseph Weizembaum[2] in the mid-1960s, which famously fooled some people some of the time, worked in exactly this way.

While it is true that ChatGPT is a hugely powerful form of memory, the answer is that nothing as simple as straightforward pattern matching could be operating here. There is pattern recognition and matching for sure, but it is much more abstract and more subtle than any simple "regurgitation" of remembered word strings would allow.

One reason that simple memory lookup will not work is that many words have multiple meanings (polysemy). This means we can only make sense of individual words by considering the context of the other words that they appear with. As we saw in Chapter 5, Elman's network did not do simple pattern matching. Instead, it was able to find grammatical structure in sentences, for instance, tracking long-distance dependencies between words (albeit while learning just a tiny fraction of human language). ChatGPT's proficiency in language, including its capacity to interpret words in context, tells us that it cannot be doing simple pattern-matching either. Instead, it is abstracting away from the literal text to find the deep structure that represents how words come together to express ideas (we will explore this further in relation to other AIs in what follows). Elman was able to show that his network was learning the hidden structure of language. ChatGPT is doing the same thing writ large. The task of understanding how ChatGPT solves language has barely begun—we do not yet have a theory of language here—but we do have an existence proof for the possibility of artificial language use that goes well beyond pattern-matching on superficial resemblance.

Another reason to doubt whether any kind of brute force approach would work is that the search space for language is vast. The mathematician Steven Wolfram[3] discusses the idea of simply storing how often words occur together in sequences of different lengths, called *n-grams*. Wolfram estimates that there are around forty thousand words in common use in English; however, when you look at pairs of words, or 2-grams, about which a full language model might store statistics, there are already around 1.5 billion. When you go to 3-grams, there are nearly sixty trillion. As you approach the length of a typical sentence (fifteen to twenty words), the number of possible combinations becomes astronomic. Remember how, in Chapter 4, we saw that the search space for chess had more states that there are atoms in the known universe? The same is true in spades for language.

Finally, if we compare ChatGPT to the human brain, then its size—175 billion parameters—looks modest. This amounts to less than one-fifth of 1% of the total estimated size of the human connectome (one hundred trillion connections). For Broca's area alone, an area known to be involved in processing language, including grammar, a conservative estimate would put this at 1.5 trillion connections, almost ten times the size of ChatGPT 3.5. If you think that deep AIs are leveraging immense memory capacity and processing power to solve language, then they are simply following nature's example.

DO AIs UNDERSTAND?

It is a common critique of AI systems that they merely process symbols using rules and have no understanding of what anything means (recall Searle's "Chinese Room" thought experiment from Chapter 2). So, do LLMs, like ChatGPT, capture the meaning of words? The answer is both yes and no.

Philosophers of language, beginning with Gottlob Frege,[4] who we encountered in Chapter 4 as one of the founders of logic, distinguish between the *sense* of a word and its *referent*. Sense relates to the mental content of a word, including its relationship to other words. For example, words often occur in clusters—dogs, cats, rabbits, and goldfish, for instance, are part of a cluster we might refer to as pets. Words also gain their sense through their relationship with words they are similar to (synonyms) or the opposite of (antonyms). The sense of a word also depends on the wider context in which it appears—the passage of text surrounding a word is often important to disambiguate the meaning of that word. ChatGPT and similar LLMs acquire a lot of knowledge about the relationships between words, as demonstrated by their ability to answer questions relating to semantic categories, synonyms/antonyms, and so on, and to correctly interpret ambiguous words in context. To this extent, LLMs clearly know a great deal about meaning in relation to sense.

On the other hand, the referent, according to Frege, describes the object, or objects, in the world that a word or expression refers to. For example, the sentence "the Arctic Monkeys are a rock band from Sheffield" describes an actual rock band, the Arctic Monkeys, and the city they originated from, Sheffield in England. ChatGPT can tell you a lot about Sheffield, including its geographical location, history, and culture, and about the Arctic Monkeys, including that they were formed in Sheffield in 2002. However, this all has to do with sense— the relationships of these words to other words—ChatGPT has no knowledge of the referents at all. If you have never heard the music of the Arctic Monkeys, you could only ever claim to know about them; you would not know them as a music listener does. If you have never been to Sheffield, then you do not really know Sheffield either (so you should visit!). ChatGPT is in a similar position, except many times worse. An LLM has never heard any music, never mind the kind of indie-rock, post-punk music that was emerging in the North of England in the early 2000s. More generally, ChatGPT has no first-hand experience of anything. Everything that the model knows about the meaning of words has simply to do with how words relate to other words. What is surprising with LLMs is how far you can get based on sense alone; it is truly astonishing that ChatGPT can discuss complex ideas so fluently without reference.

We have focused here on LLMs, but progress is also being made in other domains, for instance, image generation, where models such as *Midjourney* and *Dall-E* are able to generate images from text prompts (as discussed further in what follows). These models again make use of the ability to scrape large volumes of training data from the internet; in this case, images that have been captioned by human viewers. In this kind of AI, the base system learns about images and text together in a single model. These models encode the relationship between language and a very different domain, visual images, which shows one of the ways in which words can gain meaning. For instance, an image-generating AI, such as Dall-E, knows the word "chair", but it can also generate images of what chairs look like. This may not be reference in the full sense—an image of a chair is still not a chair—but there are more elements of chair-ness now than before.

By learning these kinds of joint representations, AIs can explicitly link the sense of words to many kinds of non-linguistic data. Music-generating AIs are now able to listen to a song and generate new music in a similar style. Connect this music-generating AI to a language AI, and now the combined system can know about the Arctic Monkeys and something more about their music. Such an AI could, for instance, say something useful about the musical similarity between the Arctic Monkeys and other post-punk bands.

Combine language, video, and audio in one AI, and you start to have an intelligent multimodal language and memory system that has increased similarity to the one inside your head. Recall the cortical association areas mentioned in Chapter 2 (and illustrated in Figure 2.2). Many of these are strongly multimodal. For instance, a region of the parietal association area, called LIP, combines visual, auditory, somatosensory, and vestibular (inner ear) signals, putting them into a common reference frame that can be used to guide movement through the environment.[5] Recent advances in AI, such as the multimodal image-generating models, are starting to show how this can be done.

Is this meaning, though? The philosopher Stevan Harnad,[6] building on John Searle's Chinese Room thought experiment, would argue that the representations in all these generative AIs are still not *grounded*. The reason is that the interpretation of their output—images, text, sound, and so forth—is ultimately in the mind of the observer (the user of the AI) and not in the machine. After all, on one level, these AIs are just manipulating huge arrays of numbers according to very complex rules. This looks a lot like Searle in the Chinese room manipulating meaningless squiggles. Is there anything here that is equivalent to human meaning?

As discussed at the start of this book, people are intelligent, not their brains. Brains are full of vast patterns of electrical activity, with brain cells communicating via electrical spikes and chemistry, so it is hard to see meaning there, too, especially if you simply look inside. For many philosophers of language, following Frege, meaning is relational—it arises when you consider the person and their interaction with the world and with other people.

This brings us to our next topic, the importance of acting in the world for grounding meaning in AI.

BODIES AND EXTENDED MINDS

Is there a way to make AI so that it has genuine understanding of the world and so that the language it uses has referents in the same way as human language use? Yes, there probably is, and it is to give AI a body in the form of a robot.

Intelligence in biological organisms exists in embodied systems in which an embedded nervous system interacts with the world through the medium of a body. Whilst humans serve as an existence proof for embodied general intelligence, there is no natural model of what a fully disembodied intelligence could look like. Therefore, we do not know if intelligence without a body is even possible.

Being embodied is important for human intelligence for several reasons.

First, most of what the brain does involves the close coupling of perception with action to perform appropriate behaviours in the world that are temporally and spatially organised and goal-directed. This is also the meaning of intelligence in its broader sense, as discussed in Chapter 2.

Our bodies also help to make some of the problems that the brain needs to solve easier. For example, our ability as two-footed animals (bipeds) to walk and run on uneven surfaces relies as much on the mechanical design of our legs and feet as on the neural circuits that control their movement. For instance, the arches of the foot, together with the sole, tendons, and ligaments, provide natural shock absorption that allows energy to be absorbed on contact with the ground and then released as the foot lifts off. At the same time, the flexibility of the toes and the articulation of the ankle play an important role in maintaining balance. The elegant and intricate design of the human foot, described by Leonardo da Vinci as both "a masterpiece of engineering and a work of art",[7] contributes to the exceptional stability and energy efficiency of human walking and running, which is unmatched in contemporary robots.

Humans, as a technological species, are also highly adept at exploiting the world and shaping it as an *extension* of our intelligence. For instance, as noted earlier, the philosopher Andy Clark has discussed how we offload some of the work of thinking to external tools such as pen and paper, a calculator, or a computer. We also integrate external devices, such as prosthetic limbs, musical instruments, cars, and bicycles, as extensions to our bodies. Language serves as an additional form of cognitive extension that is both internal (inner speech) and external (shared with others) and so serves to scaffold and accelerate our thinking and problem-solving.

THE TOTAL TURING TEST

Embodiment and the coordination of perception with action are so important in human intelligence that an alternative to the Turing test has been proposed in which the challenge is not simply to match human linguistic capability in a disembodied conversational setting but to replicate our robotic capacity as well. In other words, in addition to being able to communicate like a person, to pass the "total Turing test"[8] proposed by Stevan Harnad, AI should also be able to act in the world as a person might do.

Whilst there is no imminent prospect of a robot passing the total Turing test, the field of robotics has made significant strides towards creating forms of human-like embodied intelligence. Robots can now walk and sometimes run on two legs. They can build maps and navigate environments, grasp, fetch, carry, and manipulate objects. Current robots lack the agility, dexterity, and robustness of humans, but the gap is closing.

Researchers in robotics have found that layered control architectures that combine a mixture of fast but inflexible and slower but more deliberative processes may work best for creating robot intelligence. In other words, these architectures are starting to resemble what we find in the human brain (see Chapter 3). Robotic systems also require more of the control-style building blocks we encountered in Chapter 4, predictive control being increasingly important, as discussed in what follows.

Would an embodied AI that could pass this total Turing test understand the world in the fullest sense of that word? A robot embedded in an environment and interacting with it should certainly be able to grasp the referents of language more successfully than a disembodied AI. For a bipedal robot, for example, a chair, in addition to being something that it could recognise and name, would be a physical object it could move, lift, knock over, sit on, or fall off. In other words, the chair would have multiple possibilities for action for a robot biped, just as it would for a person.

Success in the total Turing test should also be more resistant to the philosophical challenge of the Chinese Room. As Harnad writes,

> Searle's argument fails logically for the robot version of the Turing Test, for in simulating it [the robot] he [Searle] would either have to use its transducers and effectors (in which case he would not be simulating all of its functions) or he would have to be its transducers and effectors, in which case he would indeed be duplicating their causal powers (of seeing and doing).[9]

As AI becomes increasingly capable of acting in the real world without human mediation, it may become more difficult to sustain any claim that AI is just simulating intelligence and is not a form of actual intelligence.

SCALING UP TO ARTIFICIAL GENERAL INTELLIGENCE

Most existing AIs are narrow in that they attempt to solve just one problem and be good at that one thing, be it playing chess, computing the shape of a protein, speculating on the financial markets, or being a chatbot. But are current AIs progressing towards a more general form of intelligence?

OpenAI, the creators of ChatGPT, certainly think so. Their ambition is to create artificial general intelligence, and building LLMs can be seen as an important step in that direction. Indeed, they have already shown that ChatGPT can be used as the internal engine of AIs targeting specific language challenges. For instance, with a relatively small amount of additional supervised training, such extended models can support a range of language tasks, including summarising, question-answering, and text-based games.[10] However, ChatGPT still describes itself as a "general-purpose language AI" rather than as an AGI, which seems about right.

The transformer architecture that underlies LLMs has been shown to be effective in other domains besides language. For instance, transformers are now being combined with convolutional neural networks (CNNs) to solve problems in vision. But transformers and CNNs are just two of the tools in the box. AI developers, as we reviewed in Chapter 4, have many approaches they can use.

For instance, a probabilistic method known as *diffusion* modelling[11] is currently proving useful in image- and video-generating AIs. Diffusion models are a form of generative AI in which the data in a complex pattern is gradually and systematically degraded, thereby turning it into a simple pattern of pure noise. Meanwhile, the AI learns to reverse this process—going from a simple pattern with no structure to a detailed and complex pattern (see Figure 6.1, top).

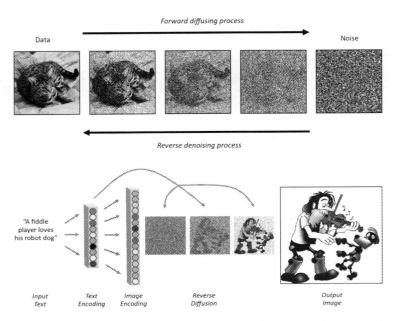

Figure 6.1 *Top.* Diffusion models use unsupervised learning to determine the underlying structure of data (here, an image of a cat). Two separate processes work in different directions to systematically degrade the pattern and to reconstruct (denoise) the pattern. The process in each direction occurs over hundreds of steps, adding/removing a small amount of noise at each step. *Bottom.* Diffusion used in text-to-image generation. Neural networks convert the text into a text encoding and then into an image encoding. The reverse diffusion process then constructs a possible image. The arrows at the top of the figure illustrate that the text encoding is used in the reverse diffusion process. This image was created with OpenAI's Dall-E 2, in which the diffusion model, which has 3.5 billion parameters, is trained with both image and text data.[12]

Diffusion AI is learning how to remove noise from images, known as *denoising*. However, like other generative models, we end up with a model that is much more powerful than this suggests—in order to denoise, the network must learn about the underlying structure of complex visual scenes. AIs such as *MidJourney* and OpenAI's *Dall-E* combine diffusion modelling with other neural networks that learn the relationship between text and images as noted previously. This creates a combined model that can create a novel image based on a text description. This is illustrated for the text input "a fiddle player loves his robot dog" in Figure 6.1 (bottom).

The success of generative AI has led to new theories of brain function. The *predictive processing* approach,[13] building on earlier theories of predictive learning, such as the Rescorla-Wagner rule, proposes that neural networks in the cerebral cortex construct predictive models of the world, which are then compared against sensory inputs. A more ambitious theory, developed by Karl Friston,[14] proposes that organisms, including humans, can be understood as implicit generative models of their environment that seek to minimise the disparity or surprise between the predictions they make and the sensory signals they receive. This is also reminiscent of Ashby's law, that we encountered in Chapter 2, that a machine must be at least as complex as the system it controls if it is to be stable in the face of change.

Whilst the predictive processing approach suggests that there are deep common principles shared between current theories of the brain and successful modelling approaches in AI, by itself, this may not be sufficient to allow us to build AGI.[15] This takes us back to the problem of architecture that we discussed in Chapter 3. How do you construct a complete working system with multiple component parts, some of them narrow AIs, that has the skills and flexibility to do all the tasks humans currently do?

One way to scale AI towards general intelligence may be to combine machine learning approaches with other forms of reasoning, as discussed in Chapter 5. For example, although ChatGPT can attempt logical puzzles and generate linguistic output that is usually coherent, it is not specifically able to do logical reasoning as, for instance, a theorem proving AI might do. This is also one of the reasons that this kind of AI cannot be relied upon to give entirely trustworthy answers.

More broadly, a wide range of computational processes, mathematics being one example, have their own internal logic, which cannot be accurately captured by a learning machine such as a transformer network. Steven Wolfram[16] describes these sorts of processes as *computationally irreducible*. In deriving a theorem in maths, for example, you cannot simply replace a long series of steps with a shortcut arrived at through learning and expect to always get the right answer. ChatGPT may get it right a lot of the time, and training with technical content can make it better; however, ChatGPT is not solving maths and engineering challenges from first principles, so you would not want to use it to pilot a plane or build a bridge.

One way ahead is clear, though. AIs like ChatGPT, which have acquired powerful capabilities such as the ability to converse in natural language, can be combined with systems designed specifically for formal reasoning. For instance, Steven Wolfram recently announced a ChatGPT plug-in for his mathematical and computational reasoning system, *Wolfram Alpha*, that provides exactly this kind of extension.

Human thinking is also fallible, and our brains are probably more like transformer networks than theorem-proving machines. To do the computationally irreducible parts of thinking, we partly rely on language, which serves as an internal mechanism for some kinds of reasoning, together with external tools such as notebooks, calculators, and computers. When making important decisions, we know from experience not to always trust our initial best guess as the right thing to do, so we work through the possibilities in a more deliberative fashion, making sure we have considered all the pros and cons. When we are doing this, our minds are sometimes in full-on internal dialogue mode as a way of compactly representing and reasoning about complex ideas. Deliberative reasoning is not just linguistic though— think of Einstein imagining a falling lift or an engineer picturing the design of a new bridge—visuospatial and bodily-kinaesthetic reasoning (imagining possible actions) are important too. Within our brains, neural networks operating in multiple modalities and specialised towards different kinds of pattern generation, internal simulation, and reasoning interact, share knowledge, and apply multiple strategies to solve hard problems. We are a considerable way off from building an AGI that can do all these things.

DIFFERENT KINDS OF INTELLIGENCE

Let us return to one of the questions from the beginning of this book. Is there one kind of intelligence or many?

One thing we have learned is that there are powerful machine learning algorithms that can solve problems that hitherto only humans could solve. Some of these algorithms, particularly deep neural networks, have interesting similarities to the brain, especially with neural circuits in the cerebral cortex. AIs that employ deep learning solve problems by constructing distributed internal representations, some of which involve the decomposition of patterned data into features at different levels of abstraction. This appears to be a fundamental building block of intelligence. A second type of general learning system can find structure in sequential data, such as speech or language, by utilising recurrent connectivity or selective attention.

Increasingly, AI is focusing on generative systems that are trained to reproduce their own inputs and, in doing so, discover hidden structures in high-dimensional pattern spaces. This capability allows them to generate new outcomes that have never been seen before. Having acquired this kind of knowledge, specific tasks that make use of it can be learned quickly. Research in understanding human intelligence has increasingly explored generative models to understand the computations happening in the brain, particularly those involving cortical microcircuits, so this appears to be a powerful strategy for constructing AI that is also shared with biological intelligence.

On the other hand, we have also seen that different types of AI may be best suited to different types of problems. For instance, some aspects of intelligence may not be computationally reducible to pattern recognition-type problems. Tasks such as logical reasoning or problem-solving, for instance, may be intrinsically serial and require coordination of multiple brain systems. This idea also supports Daniel Kahneman's idea of fast and slow thinking—fast thinking corresponds to acquired pattern recognition abilities whose workings are not consciously accessible, and slow thinking, being more deliberative and sequential, requires conscious effort and is scaffolded by our language skills and the extended mind. The typical adult human brain also has many highly specialised parts adapted towards different functions. We also see qualitatively different forms of learning in brain areas such as the cortex and the cerebellum and in circuits involving the basal ganglia.

In conclusion, then, the picture is nuanced. There is evidence for generic capacities that underly multiple forms of intelligence and a need for bespoke specialised systems in different domains. The power of machine learning algorithms also suggests learning from experience is critical for constructing intelligence; taken together with evidence of the learning capacity of children, this counters suggestions that our potential for intelligent action is determined before we are born.

Of the different kinds of intelligence discussed in Chapter 2, two stand out as not being addressed in current AI systems—*intrapersonal* and *interpersonal* intelligence—the abilities to understand oneself and others. These capacities are undoubtedly related. Indeed, one reason that AIs have yet to develop social intelligence is that to understand and relate to others, you first need to know something about yourself.[17] Existing AIs, even super-powerful systems such as ChatGPT, have no such self-awareness. Indeed, the notion of being anything at all is meaningless to current AIs. We will see in Chapter 7 that this is also relevant in considering the emerging societal risks posed by AI. Our tendency to anthropomorphise AIs—seeing them as entities with a self-concept and a concern for their futures—may be getting in the way of understanding the potential of AI for both good and bad.

In summary, we have seen that the AIs we have today are narrow and that the dream of developing AGI is some way off. Partly because we have yet to solve the problem of cognitive architecture (assembling multiple component AIs into a larger intelligent system) and partly because current AIs are not sufficiently immersed in the world to have grounded representations. It is likely that some elements of human intelligence, such as scientific discovery and aspects of creativity and imagination, will remain beyond AI until these challenges have been addressed.

HUMANS AS CYBER-PHYSICAL SYSTEMS

In 1976, Alan Newell and Herbert Simon, two of the founders of AI, were presented with the Turing Award—a kind of "Nobel prize" for computer science—for their work in AI, and particularly for the development of the *General Problem Solver*, an AI that could solve puzzles and reasoning problems via heuristic search. In their award acceptance paper,[18] Newell and Simon proposed what they considered to be a general law of intelligent systems that they named the "Physical Symbol System Hypothesis". A physical symbol system, or PSS, is a machine that stores and manipulates symbols and structures composed of symbols (as discussed in Chapter 3), a useful example being a general-purpose computer. The PSS hypothesis proposes that "a physical symbol system has the necessary and sufficient means for general intelligent action". By "general intelligent action", Newell and Simon meant actions that would be seen as intelligent when performed by people. By "sufficient", they meant that being a physical symbol system of adequate size and appropriately programmed should be enough to exhibit general intelligence, and by "necessary", they meant that all intelligent entities, including humans, must be physical symbol systems.

As a hypothesis, Newell and Simon's proposal was intended to be tested and possibly refuted. The programs of research in AI and cognitive science over the past fifty years can be seen partly as just that—an effort to see if computers could produce general intelligence and to find out whether human and animal intelligence should be viewed as symbol processing. The outcome of these programs has been to create a variety of forms of AI, as reviewed in this book, but also to identify several critical challenges to the PSS hypothesis, many of which we have also discussed in the preceding pages.

These challenges include that the core processes underlying intelligence are subsymbolic rather than symbolic, as discussed in Chapter 5; that processing in symbol systems is essentially meaningless, as discussed in the current chapter; and that processing in intelligent systems such as humans is not computational at all. This latter claim has been made on a variety of grounds, one being that the brain should be understood as a dynamical system (as discussed in Chapter 3) and not as a computational one (a computational system is a special case of a dynamical system). Another argument often made is that there is something fundamentally and qualitatively different about biological intelligence that can only be captured by considering what is happening at the level of neurochemistry or even quantum physics. This argument is typically made by people who are critical of functionalism, such as John Searle, and who consider that two systems as fundamentally different in their physical make-up as brains and computers cannot possibly be doing something equivalent.

As we have explored in this book, several of these arguments have merit. In particular, the success of machine learning has moved the field of AI away from classical symbol processing and towards the area of large-scale, hugely distributed systems that process numerical data according to principles derived from probability theory and so on. However, the argument between symbolic and subsymbolic AI is not an argument against functionalism itself or against the idea of intelligence being computation. This has been an argument within the computationalist camp about the *style* of computation that underlies intelligence. On both sides, similar ideas prevail about the importance of computational processes, such as search and optimisation, in making intelligence possible.

What makes intelligence computational rather than merely dynamical? All physical systems that change over time—the climate, the solar system, our bodies, and our brains—are dynamical systems. Why should intelligent systems be considered as a special case? One reason is that we find, in computers and in brains, coding schemes that have some universality. Computers use a digital code, whereas brains use a hybrid code that mixes digital and analogue elements, as discussed in Chapter 3. Computation in the brain is different from either digital or analogue computation, but it is still computation in a generic sense in that the brain's internal code employs representational primitives built around the spiking activity of neurons. This code is employed throughout the nervous system to process information from different modalities and to perform operations related to sensing, decision-making, and action. Dynamical systems do not routinely employ codes; computational ones do.

One problem for anti-functionalists and those who think there is something uniquely special about biological intelligence is that AI has made substantial, if uneven, progress in mastering challenges that we thought were the exclusive domain of biological intelligence. Although there is some way to go to create general intelligence, we now have machines that outperform or match humans on many traditional measures of specific intelligence. A further problem for the anti-functionalist camp is that alternative proposals for the nature of intelligence are running a very poor second. Artificial entities that display intelligence generally exploit computation in one form or another.

One of the strongest criticisms that has been levelled at the PSS hypothesis is that processing in computers is meaningless. However, as we have explored in this chapter, there is a path to bringing meaning into AI and that is via embodiment and grounding. This requires placing AIs into richer two-way interactions with their environments, for instance, via robotic bodies.

Since the mid-2000s, engineers have been thinking about complex physical systems that integrate software and hardware and interact on multiple levels with each other and the world, using the term *cyber-physical systems*.[19] Cyber-physical systems are composed of multiple embedded processors, sensors, actuators, and other electromechanical parts, such that their computational and physical elements are deeply intertwined. As illustrated in Figure 6.2, these systems use high-bandwidth communications to network with other cyber-physical systems such that computation is not confined to one physical device.

Cyber-physical systems, as studied by engineers, include highly distributed entities such as smart grids and factory automation systems; however, the concept also applies to integrated self-contained entities such as autonomous vehicles and robots. For many of these systems, distributed embedded processing, the capacity for real-time

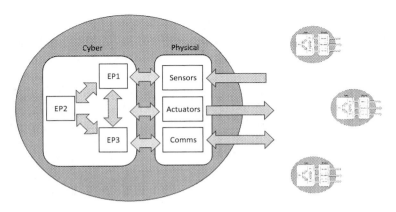

Figure 6.2 A cyber-physical system contains embedded processors that are deeply entwined with the physical elements of the broader system, including sensor and actuator sub-systems. They engage in high-bandwidth communication with other such systems. EP= embedded processor, Comms= communications.

control, and rich multimodal interaction with the environment is of central importance.

One possibility for a general principle for intelligence is to replace Newell and Simon's physical symbol system hypothesis with a *cyber-physical system hypothesis*. In other words, to consider that being a cyber-physical system is necessary and sufficient for intelligent action.[20] If this hypothesis has merit, then rather than thinking of the brain as a special sort of symbol-processing computer, we should reconceive the nervous system as a network of embedded processors. These processors perform computation, but not necessarily of the symbolic kind, are embedded within a wider physical system, that is, the whole body, and are highly networked with other such systems— people, animals, and smart machines.

If humans and robots are both cyber-physical systems, then it is reasonable to ask whether this means we are biological robots. In a functional sense, we probably are. But function is not everything, and our biological constitution makes us materially different from any robot that has ever been built or that ever could be built. We are also evolved beings, which means we possess the biological imperative—the drive to survive—that we share with other living things but is absent from human-made artefacts.

NOTES

1 From the "Marcus on AI" blog, retrieved from https://garymarcus.substack.com/p/noam-chomsky-and-gpt-3

2 Weizenbaum, J. (1976). *Computer Power and Human Reason: From Judgment to Calculation*. New York: Penguin Books.

3 Wolfram, S. (2023). *What is ChatGPT doing . . . and Why Does it Work?* Champaign, IL: Wolfram Media Inc.

4 Frege, G. (1892). On Sense and Reference [Über Sinn und Bedeutung]. *Zeitschrift für Philosophie und philosophische Kritik*, 100(1892), 25–50.

5 Andersen, R. A. (1997). Multimodal integration for the representation of space in the posterior parietal cortex. *Philosophical Transactions of the Royal Society of London. Series B: Biological Sciences*, 352(1360), 1421–1428.

6 Harnad, S. (1989). Minds, machines, and Searle. *Journal of Experimental and Theoretical AI*, 1, 5–25.

7 DeSilva, J., McNutt, E., Benoit, J., & Zipfel, B. (2019). One small step: A review of Plio-Pleistocene hominin foot evolution. *American Journal of Physical Anthropology*, 168(S67), 63–140.

8 Harnad (1989).

9 Ibid.

10 Radford, A., Wu, J., Child, R., Luan, D., Amodei, D., & Sutskever, I. (2018). Language models are unsupervised multitask learners. *OpenAI Blog*.

11 Sohl-Dickstein, J., Weiss, E. A., Maheswaranathan, N., & Ganguli, S. (2015). Deep unsupervised learning using nonequilibrium thermodynamics. *arXiv*, 1503.03585v03583.

12 Ramesh, A., Dhariwal, P., Nichol, A., Chu, C., & Chen, M. (2022). Hierarchical text-conditional image generation with CLIP latents. *arXiv*, 2204.06125v1.

13 Clark, A. (2013). Whatever next? Predictive brains, situated agents, and the future of cognitive science. *Behavioural & Brain Sciences*, 36(3), 181–204.

14 Friston, K. (2010). The free-energy principle: a unified brain theory? *Nature Reviews Neuroscience*, 11, 127.

15 Prescott, T. J., & Wilson, S. P. (2023). Understanding brain functional architecture through robotics. *Science Robotics*, 8(78), eadg6014.

16 Wolfram (2023).

17 Prescott, T. J., & Camilleri, D. (2019). The synthetic psychology of the self. In M. I. Ferreira et al. (Eds.), *Cognitive Architectures* (pp. 85–104). Cham: Springer.

18 Newell, A., & Simon, H. A. (1976). Computer science as empirical inquiry: symbols and search. *Commun. ACM*, 19(3), 113–126.

19 Rajkumar, R. (2012). A cyber–physical future. *Proceedings of the IEEE (Special Centennial Issue)*, 1309–1312.

20 This idea arose in discussion with the control and dynamical systems theorist John Doyle.

7

LIVING WITH ARTIFICIAL INTELLIGENCE

Our human lives are increasingly impacted by AI. Sometimes directly, for instance, when we interact with a device such as a mobile phone, chatbot, or robot vacuum cleaner. More often, it is indirect, as more and more of the services we use, hospitals, banks, and so on, and the cultural media that we access—music, TV, art, literature—leverage the increasing power of AI. These impacts create a new role for psychology: understanding how people will interact with AI and ensuring that these interactions are beneficial and not damaging. One name for this research domain is *human-machine interaction*; another is *user experience*,[1] often abbreviated to UX. In this chapter, we will look briefly at this emerging field before considering some broader societal and ethical questions around the emergence of AI.

USER EXPERIENCE AND HOW WE SEE AIs

UX research explores human factors—how to make systems that are safe for people to use, with user-friendly interfaces, and with personalisation of designs to meet individual needs. Psychological research is also exploring how to make AI technologies more beneficial to humans, for instance, in the form of personal assistants, in education through intelligent tutoring, or in robotics through assistive robots

DOI: 10.4324/9781003088660-7

and prosthetic devices. In therapeutic settings, AI also has the potential to augment existing mental health treatments, such as cognitive behavioural therapy, aspects of which are now being delivered by AI-based tools.

In the case of AIs embedded in chatbots, avatars, smart speakers, and robots, research is also exploring the extent to which human behaviour and attitudes towards AIs resemble or differ from behaviour towards other humans. In my research group, for example, we have explored how attitudes towards social robots can change through direct interactions and also indirectly—for example, when a friend interacts with a robot and then tells you about it.[2] This type of attitude change resembles a dynamic that happens in human relationships, where how you feel about a third person can change based on the opinion of someone you know and trust.

UX research is also concerned with the interaction between the human user and an AI and how this might unfold over time. For example, should an AI mimic a human in how it looks and sounds, or should we intentionally design interfaces and behaviour to be more machine-like?[3]

Research exploring how people see AIs has found that people are often very quick to think of these kinds of technologies as social others. For instance, in the 1990s, Byron Reeves and Clifford Nass, in an influential book called *The Media Equation*,[4] showed that people behave towards devices such as computers and televisions as they would towards other humans. Specifically, they found that people follow social norms when interacting with these technologies, such as being polite, and attribute human characteristics to such devices, including friendliness, sense of humour, and emotion. In one study, participants were asked to rate a computer terminal as to whether it was good or bad at its task. Reeves and Nass found that people provided more positive ratings if they were making their judgements via the same computer they had used to perform that task, compared to when they provided ratings through a second computer. It was as though people were anxious to avoid hurting the computer's feelings by providing negative feedback but were happy to give a frank assessment through a different machine. Contemporary attitudes towards media devices may be less deferential!

The tendency to project human-like attributes onto animals or machines is termed anthropomorphism. An experiment performed by Fritz Heider and Marianne Simmel[5] in 1944 showed that people see human-like behaviour and intentions in something as minimal as an animation of geometric figures such as circles and triangles. In other words, the tendency to anthropomorphise may be so natural for us that it is impossible to avoid seeing artefacts as similar to us if they appear to have agency or to act with any intelligence.

One conclusion you might draw from this is that we should design AIs and similar machines to make use of anthropomorphism on the basis that this will make our interactions more intuitive. An alternative school of thought holds that intentionally making a machine appear human-like is a form of deception since AIs cannot be humans, so any pretence in that direction is ethically wrong. However, deception is not unique to AI; the pacifiers and dolls that we provide to our children also have positive effects by standing in for something human. When we enjoy theatre and cinema, we also willingly suspend disbelief and accept a degree of pretence. How we perceive AIs and robots may be similarly complex in that we are able to simultaneously conceive of these technologies as tools and as social others.[6]

HUMAN-AI RELATIONSHIPS

One important question is whether treating AIs as social entities will lead to people forming relationships with them and, if so, where that might take us. The writer and social scientist Sherry Turkle[7] has warned that forming relationships with machines could be damaging, as it could lead to people having fewer secure and fulfilling relationships with each other. However, the risks of people becoming over-attached to AIs should be weighed against the potential benefits of artificial companionship.[8] Although AIs cannot provide friendship in the same way as other humans, not all the relationships we find valuable are symmetrical. For instance, people form rewarding bonds with non-human others, such as animal pets. In an age when many people describe their lives as lonely, there may be value in having AI companionship as a form of reciprocal social interaction that is stimulating and personalised. Human loneliness is often characterised by a downward spiral in which isolation leads to lower self-esteem, which discourages further interaction with people. There may be ways in which AI companionship could help break this cycle by scaffolding feelings of self-worth and helping maintain or improve social skills. If so, relationships with AIs could support people to find companionship with human and artificial others.

An alternative to the deception view of anthropomorphism in AI is to step back from worrying about the essential nature of AIs as compared to humans and to consider this as a more practical matter grounded in how people see machines. What matters ethically, perhaps, has more to do with the patterns and consequences of our social interactions, including their meaning and significance to the people involved and the wider consequences of those interactions for our other relationships.

In the end, this also very much depends on who is designing the AIs and for what purpose. An increasing risk is that AIs, like some existing social media, will be designed to encourage users to interact for longer and longer periods and to keep them coming back. This has less to do with the capabilities of the AI systems themselves and more to do with how the companies that develop the AI are choosing to deploy them. It is, therefore, important that psychologists and other social scientists critically examine the emergence of human-AI relationships and their societal consequences to identify the potential risks and benefits. Some regulation may be needed to mitigate risks and prevent harm.

BIAS AND ERROR IN AI

Discussions of AI risk frequently highlight the problem of bias in AI systems. As more and more areas of life employ AI technology to systematise and streamline processes and reduce loads on human workers, the presence of bias in any such system could cause significant harm.

For example, in job recruitment, AIs are being used to select which job adverts people see and, once they have applied for a job, to sort through applications and determine who should be shortlisted. In one example, a tool for targeted advertising of job vacancies developed by Google was found to preferentially target men rather than women for higher-paid jobs.[9] This kind of bias is not inherent in the machine learning algorithm; rather, it is inherited from the training data, which in many cases is collected automatically by scraping the internet. Sadly, but not surprisingly, an AI trained to identify what sort of people should be highly paid would likely infer, from current levels of gender inequality in pay, that the most suitable candidates for well-paid jobs will be men. Positive action that can counter such trends includes greater diligence in selecting and curating training data. Developers can also create synthetic data to improve balance or modify training sets to ensure that well-paid men and women are equally represented. Of course, human judgement can be biased too. In some settings, AI could offer a path towards more equitable decision-making, but only if we get it right.

Bias is related to the wider problem of error in AI. Large language models, for instance, are known to give responses that may be factually wrong or entirely fictional ("hallucinated"). We should not be surprised by this as the core system in an AI chatbot, such as ChatGPT, is not trained to be a fact checker; it simply generates appropriate sequences of words that follow what has come before. Any fact-checking or other forms of caution must be part of the wrapper that goes around the inner model. Given the size of the model and that it is composed of billions of numerical parameters, it is simply impossible to look inside the ChatGPT engine and accurately diagnose where it is going wrong. The current AI technology for this model is essentially a black box. That silver-tongued AIs can be misleading may be something that we have to get used to as we learn to use these tools more critically.

It may also be possible to use AI to fix AI. For instance, AI developers are using adversarial designs to make AIs work better. In an adversarial system, one AI is trained to analyse the output or behaviour of a second AI and to provide feedback to that AI based on its critique. For instance, a summary-writing AI might be linked to an editor AI that checks the summaries provided and asks for improvement or revisions. A 2023 study by Jenny Yang and colleagues[10] found that this kind of adversarial machine learning could improve fairness in an AI developed to provide healthcare screening.

There is also a considerable effort underway to increase transparency in AI. This could mean designing AIs whose inner workings can be inspected more easily—some generative models make this more straightforward—or developing AIs that not only give you an answer but also explain how they obtained that answer. Human experts can also find it difficult to articulate an explanation as to why they reached a particular conclusion—this was a problem that was encountered in the 1990s in the development of AI expert systems. Where knowledge is of the pattern recognition variety, in either humans or machines, it may be difficult to put into words. Even so, AIs that are probabilistic, as many already are, can provide useful estimates of their level of certainty in any given answer. To know how likely it is that an AI has given you a correct answer is helpful, even if it falls short of a full explanation of how the conclusion was reached.

ARTIFICIAL STUPIDITY, GENIES, AND ORACLES

AIs will always make errors, not least because the world in which they operate and in which we live is not entirely predictable. Even if the error rate is very low, as usage becomes more widespread, more and more mistakes will be made. This is already a challenge in areas such as driverless cars. While driverless cars have the potential to be safer than human-driven vehicles, they are still crashing more frequently than when people are in charge, although they may already be better at avoiding fatal collisions. One area where driverless cars are challenged is in dealing with the unexpected or unusual—what researchers call "edge" or "corner" cases.[11] These are scenarios that fall outside the normal situations that you might experience during a typical day's driving—a wild animal runs into the road, or a lorry spills hot tarmac onto the lane ahead. The challenge for the narrow AIs that pilot driverless cars is that they lack the broader understanding of the world that human drivers have that allows us to make better sense of atypical situations.

What we might call artificial stupidity, then, is not just the capacity to make errors; it is that an AI's knowledge is narrowly constrained to the domain in which it was trained. It knows nothing, literally nothing, about anything wider than that. In *Moral Machines*, the ethicist Wendell Wallach[12] describes several scenarios in which deployment of narrow AIs in areas like financial decision-making and management of critical infrastructure could lead to disastrous outcomes simply because the system concerned was oblivious to the broader picture. Wallach argues that one of the ways to make AIs more trustworthy would be to provide them with the ability to perform moral reasoning, that is, to program them to consider the consequences and rights and wrongs of different courses of action in relation to human ethical principles. However, the field of machine morality is very much in its infancy. The practical challenge of integrating any kind of ethical understanding into AI has barely begun.

In his book *Superintelligence*,[13] the philosopher Nick Bostrom worries about scenarios involving narrow AIs that could threaten human existence. For instance, Bostrom imagines an AI designed to make paperclips that is given access to the machinery needed to source and process the necessary raw materials. The paperclip AI also has the capacities to reason about and overcome challenges that might impact its production capabilities. With the simple goal of making as many paperclips as possible, Bostrom suggests that such a machine could go beyond the intentions of its human designers. Particularly, it might progressively recruit more and more resources to paperclip making and enact plans to thwart anyone that tries to restrain its actions. Ultimately, Bostrom worries that such an AI could process all of planet Earth into paperclips, then expand into the solar system and beyond, still pursuing its simple but utterly pointless mission (the paperclip-using humans being long gone). This scenario might seem far-fetched, and we can imagine various ways human society could rein in an over-exuberant paperclip-making AI. Nevertheless, this illustrates an important point—the more we cede control to AIs, the more careful we should be in deciding what we want them to optimise.

One suggestion from Bostrom is that we avoid building AIs that can act in the world in an unfettered manner. Bostrom describes such AIs as "genies" by analogy with the powerful magical beings of Islamic mythology. As AI becomes increasingly powerful, the risk that genie-type AIs will, simply in implementing their programming, do something that has unforeseen and harmful impacts on humanity will only increase. As an alternative, Bostrom advocates building "oracles", which, like the legendary oracle of Ancient Greece, would not be empowered to act directly. Instead, they could operate only to answer questions posed by people.

The potential for AI oracles to do good in the world is vast. We can already see this, for instance, in domains such as medicine, where AIs are being used to help develop new treatments and to diagnose disease. These AIs will be most useful when deployed alongside people in human-AI teams, where humans devise the questions and interpret and apply the answers. For example, we can think of the endeavour to understand human impacts on the global climate as such an enterprise. The use of very large causal models of Earth's climate—AIs in the broader sense, as discussed in Chapter 4—enables us to predict better the consequences of increasing CO_2 emissions for our climate. These models can also be used to test different scenarios and to understand the long-term implications of societal decisions about, for instance, our continued use of fossil fuels. Without these models, our capacity to predict our future climate and to develop strategies to mitigate climate change would be greatly reduced. We now have the opportunity to deploy AIs to address other pressing concerns in the world today, such as wealth inequality, sustainable food production, and improving human well-being.[14]

The risks of AI stupidity—allowing narrow AIs too much control in important domains of human life—imply that to gain fuller benefits from AI we may need to build AGIs that have a broader understanding of the world and the capacity to reason about their own societal impacts. If our human capacity to understand each other is a useful guide, then such an AGI may also need to conceive of itself and reason about itself to be able to fully conceive of and reason about human others.

We should not be misled by our anthropomorphic projections into expecting that such an entity will necessarily see the world as we do and share all our concerns. It will only do so if we take great care to ensure alignment with human principles and values. A significant risk is that the current path to AGI is being set by AI corporations, whose ultimate drive is to provide profits for shareholders. This is a largely unregulated world in which the interests of the key actors building these powerful AIs may not be sufficiently aligned with those of humanity more broadly.

AN AI SINGULARITY OR RUNAWAY HUMAN INTELLIGENCE?

The notion of an AI singularity is of a moment in time when AI surpasses human intelligence, discovers the means to improve itself without human help, and accelerates into the future,[15] perhaps leaving its human forebears in the dust. In truth, AI has already surpassed humans in many respects, as we have explored in this book, but it is still behind in others, and the path ahead is difficult to foretell.

Individual human intelligence is limited by the size of the human cranium, which has been stationary at around 1.5 litres for at least the last one hundred thousand years. However, it is wrong to think of human intelligence as confined to individual brains. Our *collective intelligence* shared through the medium of language and extended by our various cultural artefacts—from clay tablets to modern computers, internet technology, and AI—has increased dramatically over that time. We are born with an enormous capacity to absorb culture through the learning potential of the cerebral cortex,[16] which means that we are also superbly adapted to make good use of these cognitive extensions.

As AI breaks new milestones, an optimistic view is that our species can continue to piggyback on the ingenuity of our own inventions. What is an advance for AI is then an advance for human intelligence too, which—having escaped the confines of the skull through language and culture—has been on its own runaway trajectory for quite some time.[17]

The development of advanced AI is also revealing more about ourselves. The mystery of how intelligence could arise at all is beginning to be explained by the self-organising and learning capabilities of AI systems that have intriguing similarities to the vast networks of biological processors that make up our nervous systems. As psychology and AI proceed, this partnership should unlock further insights into both natural and artificial intelligence. This could help answer some key questions about what it means to be human and for humans to live alongside AI.

NOTES

1 Hassenzahl, M., & Tractinsky, N. (2006). User experience—a research agenda. *Behaviour & Information Technology*, 25(2), 91–97.

2 Sarda Gou, M., Webb, T. L., & Prescott, T. (2021). The effect of direct and extended contact on attitudes towards social robots. *Heliyon*, 7(3), e06418.

3 Prescott, T. J., & Robillard, J. M. (2022). Designing assistive robots: a relational approach. In *ICCHP-AAATE 2022 Open Access Compendium* (pp. 285–292). Linz: Assoc. ICXHP.

4 Reeves, B., & Nass, C. I. (1996). *The Media Equation: How People Treat Computers, Television, and New Media Like Real People and Places*. New York: Cambridge University Press.

5 Heider, F., & Simmel, M. (1944). An experimental study of apparent behavior. *The American Journal of Psychology*, 57(2), 243–259.

6 Prescott, T. J. (2017). Robots are not just tools. *Connection Science*, 29(2), 142–149.

7 Turkle, S. (2017). *Alone Together: Why We Expect More from Technology and Less from Each Other* (3rd ed.). New York: Basic Books.

8 Prescott, T. J., & Robillard, J. M. (2021). Are friends electric? The benefits and risks of human-robot relationships. *iScience*, 24(1), 101993.

9 Is there bias in AI recruiting? Retrieved from www.verdict.co.uk/generative-ai-recruiting-bias/

10 Yang, J. et al. (2023). An adversarial training framework for mitigating algorithmic biases in clinical machine learning. *Npg Digital Medicine*, 6(1), 55.

11 Schwartz, S. (2021). Are self-driving cars really safer than human drivers? Retrieved from https://thegradient.pub/are-self-driving-cars-really-safer-than-human-drivers/

12 Wallach, W. (2008). *Moral Machines: Teaching Robots Right from Wrong*. Oxford: Oxford University Press.

13 Bostrom, N. (2014). *Superintelligence: Paths, Dangers, Strategies*. Oxford: Oxford University Press.

14 Verschure, P. F. M. J., Halloy, J., & Prescott, T. J. (2020). Sapiens 5.0: A manifesto for the development of human-AI collaboration for good. *Proceedings of the 23rd Annual Future Studies Conference*, Emirates Center for Strategic Studies, Abu Dhabi. pp. 83–110.

15 Kurzweil, R. (2005). *The Singularity is Near*. New York: Penguin Books.

16 Krubitzer, L. A., & Prescott, T. J. (2018). The combinatorial creature: cortical phenotypes within and across lifetimes. *Trends in Neurosciences*, 41(10), 744–762.

17 Prescott, T. J. (2013). The AI singularity and runaway human intelligence. In N. F. Lepora et al. (Eds.), *Biomimetic and Biohybrid Systems 2*, (pp. 438–440). Berlin: Springer.

FURTHER READING

Bostrom, N. (2014). *Superintelligence: Paths, Dangers, Strategies*. Oxford: Oxford University Press.

Clark, A. (2010). *Supersizing the Mind Embodiment, Action, and Cognitive Extension*. Oxford: Oxford University Press.

Gardner, H. (2006). *Multiple Intelligences: New Horizons*. New York: Basic Books.

Gould, S. J. (2006). *The Mismeasure of Man (Revised and Expanded)*. New York: W. W. Norton & Company.

Kahneman, D. (2011). *Thinking Fast and Slow*. New York: Penguin.

LeCun, Y., Bengio, Y., & Hinton, G. (2015). Deep learning. *Nature*, 521(7553), 436–444.

Prescott, T. J., & Robillard, J. M. (2021). Are friends electric? The benefits and risks of human-robot relationships. *iScience*, 24(1), 101993.

Wolfram, S. (2023). *What is ChatGPT doing . . . and Why Does It Work?* Champaign, IL: Wolfram Media Inc.

Printed in the United States
by Baker & Taylor Publisher Services